CAMPANIA
ART AND ARCHEOLOGY

360 COLOUR ILLUSTRATIONS
LARGE MAP OF THE REGION

TEXT BY
PATRIZIA FABBRI

BONECHI

Project and editorial conception: Casa Editrice Bonechi
Publication Manager: Monica Bonechi
Picture research: Francesco Giannoni, Maria Rosanna Malagrinò
Graphic design and cover: Maria Rosanna Malagrinò
Video layout: Fiamma Tortoli
Editing: Patrizia Fabbri, Simonetta Giorgi
Drawings and maps: Stefano Benini
Text: Patrizia Fabbri
Translation: Anthony Brierley

© Copyright by Casa Editrice Bonechi - Florence - Italy
E-mail:bonechi@bonechi.it - Internet:www.bonechi.it

Printed in Italy by
Centro Stampa Editoriale Bonechi.

Photographs from the archives of Casa Editrice Bonechi taken by A&5 Photo Studio,
Archivio Fotografico dell'Osservatorio Vesuviano, Marco Bonechi, Ferdinando Califano, Giovanni Capodilupo,
Rita Cerciello, Gianni Dagli Orti, A. Esposito-G. Di Meo, Fornass/Sparavigna, Foto Amendola, Foto Castello,
Paolo Giambone, K&B/Grimoldi, K&B/Valsecchi, Ferdinando Mainardi, MSA, Mario and Tiziana Pirone,
Sergio Riccio, Cesare Tonini.

Other photographers (the photos on the page are credited clockwise):
A&5 Photo Studio, *pages 5e, 112d;* Atlantide/Stefano Amantini, *pages 56a, 59a, 60b, 90;*
Atlantide/Massimo Borchi, *pages 75b, c, 76c, 78, 84c, 86b, 87b, 112a;*
Atlantide/Guido Cozzi, *pages 106b, 111b, 112c, 125a;*
Azienda Autonoma Soggiorno e Turismo Vico Equense/Raffaele Venturini, *page 72b;*
Gaetano Barone, *pages 4d, 33b, 57a, 58c, 63a, 66b, 76b, 79b, 102b, 108b;*
Gianni Dagli Orti, *pages 45, 51c, 52a, 53a, c-e, 54a, b, d, 55;*
Foto Scala, Firenze, *pages 17, 71b;* Foto Tripodi, *page 7;* Maurizio Fraschetti, *pages 3b, 107d, h, 111a, 112b, 113;*
Francesco Giannoni, *pages 5c, 56/57, 82, 91a, 93d, e, 107f, 118c, 120b, 122c;* K&B/Cellai, *page 12b;*
K&B/R. Peruzzi, *page 91b;* Andrea Innocenti, *pages 22b-h, 40a, 107a-c;* Mario Pirone, *pages 5d, 10c;*
Andrea Pistolesi, *pages 10d, 64b, 67, 68a, c, d, 69, 125c;*
Sergio Riccio, *pages 16, 24a, 29b;* Ghigo Roli, *pages 64a, 65a, 66c, d, 68b, 80d, 95b;*
Ufficio Stampa San Carlo/Foto Luciano Romano, *page 13.*

The Publisher is thankful to the artists Lello Esposito, Luigi Grassi *and* Vittorio Piscopo *for the permission granted for the
reproduction of the works illustrated in the box page 20.*

ISBN 88-476-0066-9

* * *

The 'Faraglioni', towering rocks rising as a symbol of
Capri. Below, ruins of the Roman Theatre at Benevento.

INTRODUCTION

The word "Campania" - which comes from "ager capuanus", the ancient name for the northern part of the plain around Capua and Naples - today designates a region that is anything but homogeneous, consisting as it does of territorial, morphological, climatic, historical and cultural realities that are highly varied and diversified. In this area, created more than a million years ago by the eruptions of the now extinct volcano of Roccamonfina, there are numerous geographical areas that are territorially, even if not administratively, well defined: the Sannio, Irpinia, the Agro Sarnese-Nocerino, the Cilento. These in turn are divided into even smaller areas that nonetheless have their own identity, such as Agro Nolano, Matese and the Amalfi coast. The most delightful plain in Italy for Strabo, Campania felix for Pliny, the region has been inhabited ever since prehistory. Industrious and culturally developed sea peoples, as well as mountain folk, flocked here, attracted by the extraordinarily mild climate, by the extreme fertility of the soil, and not at all discouraged by the considerable difficulties deriving from the volcanic na-

ture of the territory - it was no coincidence that this site was chosen by the ancients not only for the paradisiacal Elysian Fields but also for Hades. The first to come were Indo-European people of various races, then the Etruscans settled in the hinterland and founded Capua. Between the 8th and 7th century BC Greek colonists settled along the coasts and islands and established flourishing urban centres like Cumae, Parthenope and Poseidonia, the future Paestum, thus creating one of the main nuclei of Hellenic culture and civilization on the Italian peninsula. For a long time the Greeks and Etruscans fought each other, until both were suppressed by the war-like Samnites, who in turn, between the 4th and 3rd century BC succumbed to the expansion of Roman power. To the conquered Campania the Romans transmitted their laws and their culture, but also the magnificence of their urban constructions: they built theatres, baths, the aqueduct of Serino, the temples of Pozzuoli and Baia, Pompeii and Herculaneum, the great consular roads and, naturally, the luxurious and monumental villas that were just as numerous inland as they were on the rocky coasts overlooking the sea. The Romans loved Campania to the point of wanting to combine it administratively with Lazio. And it was no accident that orators and political men like Cicero and Silla, poets and philosophers like Virgil and Lucretius, and even emperors like Augustus and Tiberius, chose to spend part of their lives here and in some cases even die here. With time, and with the expansion of the Roman Empire, which led to an abundant flow onto the markets of Spanish and African goods, the agricultural economy of Campania experienced a crisis that became increasingly accentuated and resulted in the gradual abandonment of cultivated lands. When the barbarian hordes swept through southern Italy - the Visigoths of Alaric, the Ostrogoths, and the Vandals of Africa who in 456 sacked Capua - the old Campania felix appeared irremediably impoverished, the countryside dotted with marshes and racked by malaria. In 553 the Byzantines succeeded in bringing the region back under the control of the Eastern Roman Empire, but very soon after their jurisdiction remained confined to the coastal areas, where their duchies would evolve into independent cities: Naples, Gaeta, Salerno, Sorrento and Amalfi. Inland, instead, the arrival of the Longobards led to the creation of a "southern Lombardy" with its capital at Benevento. And while the Catholic Church, with the spread of monasticism, offered its own contribution to the civilization of the hinterland, new peoples - the Saracens and Normans - arrived in the area. In 1077 the Normans unified the whole of southern Italy, with the exception of Benevento, into a single state, which was later transmitted to the Swabians. The maritime cities, having lost their autonomy and having severed the privileged relations hitherto enjoyed with Byzantium, inevitably suffered an irreversible decline, while that feudal system that was destined to become a constant element in the history of Campania became widespread in the region.

After the Angevin and Aragonese interlude, the establishment of Spanish rule, with Charles V and the celebrated viceroy Pedro de Toledo, reconsigned to Naples the dual role of capital, lost in the past in favour of Palermo, and seat of the most splendid court in Italy, a veritable pole of economic, social and cultural attraction. Spurred by this authoritative revival the whole re

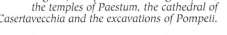

Images of Campania: archeological finds, the temples of Paestum, the cathedral of Casertavecchia and the excavations of Pompeii.

The maiolica-decorated cupola of Atrani, thriving handicrafts and the appeal of an increasingly youthful tourism, are some of the liveliest and most attractive images of present-day Campania.

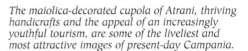

acquired new frontiers, became part of the nascent Kingdom of Italy. Naples, from capital of the Kingdom of the Two Sicilies, was relegated to the role of prefecture. Adhesion to the unified state brought with it consequences of clearly contrasting nature: on the one hand, the sacrifice of what at the time could be considered as the major Italian industries and the progressive diffusion of the scourge of unemployment; on the other, a shrewd policy of reorganization of the agricultural economy and a determined impetus given to the development of tourist infrastructures, which soon met with an enthusiastic response both at a national and international level. Even today, with an economy that is sufficiently diversified and appears to be going through a phase of recovery, tourism undoubtedly emerges as the most flourishing sector, a phenomenon favoured by the incomparable beauty of the natural surroundings and by the creative and overwhelming charm of a people who Montesquieu described as "more popular than elsewhere". And from a Naples today that seems to be waking with renewed vigour from a long period of torpor there radiates over the whole region a quiver of renewal and desire for rebirth that positively involves the economic and social sectors and seems to herald the happy recovery of ancient glories and new splendours.

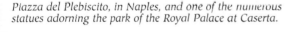

Piazza del Plebiscito, in Naples, and one of the numerous statues adorning the park of the Royal Palace at Caserta.

gion drew enormous benefits: this was seen in the Campania of Torquato Tasso and Giordano Bruno, of Marino and Basile, in the Baroque and the Catholic Reformation, which in the 18th century was replaced by the modern and enlightened Campania of Bernardo Tanucci and Giambattista Vico. This was now the Campania of the Bourbons, who succeeded the Spanish Habsburgs in 1734, after a thirty-year interlude of Austrian rule. And despite moments of obvious crisis, such as the experience of the Parthenopean Republic and the events surrounding the revolutionary movements of 1820 and 1848, the Bourbons remained on the throne until 1860, when Campania, having regained its ancient name and

View of Naples, stretched out along the homonymous gulf. In the foreground the fortified outline of Castel dell'Ovo.

NAPLES, ANCIENT CAPITAL

Naples, the principal city of southern Italy and illustrious cradle of history and art, spreads out like an amphitheatre over the slopes of the hills descending along the littoral of the homonymous gulf, between Vesuvius and the Phlegraean Fields. The city is a melting-pot of deep contradictions: here, side by side, there is great wealth and great poverty, modernity and tradition, the most majestic palaces and the lowliest of dwellings, outstanding views (from Posillipo, from Via Caracciolo, from the Museo S. Martino) and sad pockets of urban degradation, the whole being enlivened by the energetic exuberance of a people who have always, with their extraordinary resourcefulness, known how to be protagonists of the city's life.

Neapolis, the 'New City', rose near the Rhodian settlement of Parthenope and in the 5th century had already established itself as the most important centre of Campania. Surrendering to the power of Rome after the siege to which it was subjected in 327 by the consul Publilius Philon, Naples showed itself from then on to be a faithful ally of the Romans, who raised it to the status of municipium in 90 BC and to colony under the Emperor Claudius. Appreciated for its mild climate (the mean annual temperature is about 17°), for the attractions of its landscape and for its cultural features of clear Hellenistic origin (here, up until the Late Imperial Period, it prided itself on conserving its Greek language and institutions), the city was the favourite dwelling-place of Roman patricians and intellectuals (Virgil studied at the school of Syron, had a sumptuous residence and was finally buried here).

With the spread of Christianity Naples witnessed the violence of the persecutions. One of the victims was Gennarus, the bishop of Benevento, martyred at Pozzuoli in the 4th century and ever since venerated as the city's patron saint. Later, the decline of the Roman Empire would open the way for the raids of the barbarians, first among them the Ostrogoths in 493. Reconquered by the Byzantines, under new rule the city grew in wealth and power, even to the extent that it succeeded in repelling all the assaults of the Longobards and in obtaining a progressive autonomy from Byzantium, an autonomy culminating in the constitution of an independent duchy of which Naples would be capital for more than three centuries. Reduced, after the Norman conquest, to being just the main town of the Principality of Capua, with the capital of the kingdom at Palermo, and later openly siding against the Swabian dynasty that had taken over from the Normans, the city regained its old status of capital by order of the Angevins, under whose rule (1266-1442) it witnessed great urban development and a substantial cultural revival. Thus, if at the time of the Angevin conquest its inhabitants numbered no more than 40,000, at the dawn of the 16th century the population had increased to 110,000.

After the coming of the Aragonese, who for half a century vainly attempted to win popular favour, and the triumphal welcome given to Charles VIII of France in 1495, in the 16th century the city witnessed the establishment of a Spanish government that would last until 1707. Ruled by a viceroy and endowed with formal autonomy, Naples at the time knew great splendour but also equally accentuated poverty: the influx of no-

ble families that built majestic palaces in the western part of the city, the demographic development that made it the most heavily populated city in the whole of western Europe, with more than 360,000 inhabitants in 1656, and the urbanistic expansion that led to the rise of the so-called 'Spanish quarters' contrasted with the violent popular insurrections (including the celebrated Masaniello uprising of 1647), devastating epidemics of plague that decimated the population, and a progressive impoverishment caused largely by the miserly and oppressive fiscal policies of the Spanish overlords.

A progressive revival took place instead under the Bourbons, who in 1734, after a short period of Austrian rule, took power and made Naples the capital of an independent kingdom. The new rulers remained in power until 1860, with the exception of the brief interlude of the ephemeral Parthenopean Republic (1799) and by the successive rules of Joseph Bonaparte and Joachim Murat. Despite the increasingly sluggish and unprogressive rule that with time would increasingly characterize the dynasty, the Bourbon government was always fundamentally popular with the people, who benefited from its many noteworthy

With its massive trapezoidal structure, battlemented walls and imposing round towers, the Angevin Castle is an impregnable fortress that was originally ennobled by an elegant white Arco di Trionfo.

View of the sea-front of Naples, with its buildings that climb up towards the hilly hinterland.

merits, to which the flourishing of Naples, open to the culture of the Enlightenment and to progress, bore unequivocal witness: the first steamboat was built here in 1818; here, 21 years later, the first stretch of Italian railway was opened, the Naples-Portici; here the first telegraphic communications were registered; and here the fleet of the third largest navy in Europe was stationed. The city which had enchanted poets and artists like Boccaccio, Donatello, Petrarch, Caravaggio, Titian, Tasso, Milton, Shelley, Goethe and Byron, became the cradle of a new generation of intellectuals, like Francesco De Sanctis and Luigi Settembrini, and of illustrious politicians who were not extraneous to the movement of the Risorgimento, in which the city participated actively during the unfortunate insurrections of 1820 and 1848. In 1860, after the conquest of Garibaldi, Naples, together with the Kingdom of the Two Sicilies, was annexed to the Kingdom of the States of Savoy and its history thus lawfully became an integral part of the history of Italy. Among the most illustrious chapters in the city's history we should mention the epic Four Days (25-28 October 1943), by which, already exhausted by the German bombardment, it succeeded in freeing itself from Nazi oppression; one of the darkest episodes in the city's history was the violent earthquake which on 23 November 1980 devastated Irpinia, causing serious damage in the city and claiming numerous victims.

THE ANGEVIN CASTLE. Looking from here towards the sea and the harbour we can admire in all its grandeur the massive bulk of the **Angevin Castle**, named thus in honour of Charles I of Anjou, who had it built in the 13th century, but also known as *Castel Nuovo*, to distinguish it from earlier works of the city's fortification. The trapezoidal plan, the battlemented walls and the massive round towers have always contributed to giving it an appearance of impregnability. Around the middle of the 15th century, according to the wishes of Alfonso I of Aragon, the massive fortress underwent substantial rebuilding work. It was at that time that the **Arco di Trionfo** was erected between the *Torre di Mezzo* and the *Torre di Guardia*, a true masterpiece blending the elegance of Renaissance architecture and the most classical tradition of the Roman celebratory arch. The work is embellished by reliefs and sculptures executed by Francesco Laurana, Domenico Gagini and Isaia da Pisa in celebration of the virtues of Alfonso I and of his triumphal entrance into Naples. Restored several times between the 16th and 18th century and later given back its Renaissance appearance thanks to a scrupulous 20th-century restoration, the castle, which has hosted Pope Celestine V, Giotto, Petrarch, Boccaccio, Ettore Fieramosca and Charles V, is also distinguished by its extremely interesting interior, including the *courtyard* and the **church of S. Barbara**, or *Cappella Palatina*, one of the very few original parts of the Angevin period that has survived to this day.

GALLERIA UMBERTO I.

The Naples of today, the heir of an ancient and distinguished history, conserves illustrious vestiges of past and recent splendours. Note the elegant **Galleria Umberto I**, built in the very heart of the city to wipe out a whole series of infamous alleyways. The neo-Renaissance appearance given to it by Antonio Curri and Ernesto Di Mauro, who built it between 1887 and 1890 on a design by the engineer Emanuele Rocco, is perfectly in keeping with the refinement of the commercial activities it houses. The interior, with its unmistakable octagonal ground-plan, its pavement of polychrome marbles with an impressive circular decoration representing a compass and the signs of the zodiac, its barrel vaults with large windows converging on an imposing cupola, houses the city's last *Caffé chantant*, the famous "Salone Margherita".

PIAZZA DEL PLEBISCITO.

Not far from the Galleria is the splendid **Piazza del Plebiscito**, a vast, harmonious space, as elegant as an open-air salon, recently restored and closed to traffic. It lies between two monumental complexes: on one side the majestic **basilica of S. Francesco di Pao-**

The elegant Galleria Umberto I, with its unmistakable cupola, one of the most celebrated and popular places in Naples, not far from the vast open space of Piazza del Plebiscito, flanked by the austere and monumental Palazzo Reale.

la, with its enormous colonnade, designed by Leopoldo Laperuta, which reminds us of St Peter's Square in Rome, commissioned in 1817 by King Ferdinando IV (later Ferdinando I of the Two Sicilies) in recognition for the reconquered throne, and built over a period of almost thirty years on designs by the architect Pietro Bianchi in imitation of the Roman Pantheon; on the other, the moderately austere **Palazzo Reale**, started in 1600 on a design of the architect Domenico Fontana and worked on for over 50 years. The present building is the result of a whole series of modifications and renovations which over the centuries have left only the facade and the court of honour unaltered. To repair the damage caused by a fire in 1837, Gaetano Genovese made substantial modifications in the neoclassical style. Its lavish interior, where the **Biblioteca Nazionale** has had its seat since 1922, is introduced by a monumental stairway and is distinguished by the elaborate elegance of various rooms - the *Salone Centrale*, the *Sala del Trono*, the *Salone di Ercole*, and many other rooms of the **Appartamenti Reali**, now converted into a museum - by the **Cappella** and by the 18th-century **Teatrino di Corte**.

Not far away, the 19th-century **Municipio**, on the homonymous piazza dominated by the equestrian statue of Vittorio Emanuele

II, is flanked by the **church of S. Giacomo degli Spagnoli**, which Don Pedro de Toledo, viceroy of Naples, had built in the middle of the 16th century.

CASTEL DELL'OVO. Another impressive Neapolitan fortification is certainly **Castel dell'Ovo**, which is situated on the small island of Megaride in the centre of the gulf between Borgo Marinaro and the small port of Mergellina. In Roman times a fortified stronghold stood on this spot, the Castrum Lucullium, which was enlarged and reinforced in the course of the centuries by Normans and Angevins. Chosen as the royal residence by Charles I of Anjou and by Alfonso of Aragon, in the 17th century it was converted into a prison. Today it is still possible to admire the imposing structure with its ramparts built of yellow tufa, dominated by the **Torre Maestra** and the **Torre Normandia**, its alternating medieval and Gothic rooms and the celebrated **Monks' Refectory**. From its ramparts there is also an enchanting panorama over the whole Gulf of Naples. As for the rather peculiar name, this is traceable to a medieval legend according to which in one of the rooms of the castle the poet Virgil is said to have hidden an egg in a hanging jug. Legend has it that when the jug and the egg fall and shatter, the castle and the entire city will fall into ruin.

Nearby, on the sea-front, is one of the most artistic and well-known symbols of Naples, the **Fontana dell'Immacolatella**, which once stood in Piazza del Plebiscito. Splendid for the luminosity of its white and grey marbles, it was made in 1601 by Michelangelo Naccherino and Pietro Bernini.

In the centre of the Gulf, on the islet of Megaride, stands one of the most characteristic fortifications in Naples, Castel dell'Ovo. One of the most celebrated symbols of the city is the Fontana dell'Immacolatella, built in the 17th century in white and grey marble.

directly to the nearby Palazzo Reale, it was inaugurated on 4 November 1737, the king's name day. When it was destroyed by a fire in 1816, Ferdinando IV entrusted its reconstruction to Antonio Niccolini, who had it redecorated with stuccoes, gilt ornamentation and frescoes.

A splendid view of the S. Carlo Theatre and some examples of the numerous spectacles performed on its stage.

THE S. CARLO THEATRE

I n front of the Galleria stands the S. Carlo Theatre, one of the most well-loved by opera singers and orchestra conductors due to the perfection of its acoustics. Built on the orders of Charles III of Bourbon, and for the sovereign's greater ease linked

The Duomo of Naples, with its distinctive neo-Gothic facade, is dedicated to the Virgin of the Assumption, but is famous particularly for the relics of S. Gennaro housed in it.

DUOMO. One of the most important places in the life of Naples is the **Duomo**, dedicated to Our Lady of the Assumption, built on the wishes of Charles I of Anjou, or, according to other traditions, of Charles II, on the site of a 6th-century basilica known as the Stefania. Seriously damaged by an earthquake in 1349, and later, much more recently, by the German bombardments of 1943, it has several times been rebuilt, to the extent that its facade is distinguished by a clear neo-Gothic style.
In the interior, divided into a nave and two side aisles supported by 16 pilasters, there are numerous **chapels**, many of which still have their original Gothic appearance, the **apse** of 18th-century workmanship, the bishop's

throne in marble and the **tombs** of numerous illustrious men, including S. Aspreno, the first bishop of the city. Undoubtedly at the centre of popular devotion is the **Succorpo**, or *Confession of S. Gennaro*, a chapel commissioned in 1497 by Cardinal Oliviero Carafa which houses the remains of S. Gennaro, the patron saint of the city. The two flasks containing the blood of the martyr, displayed to the public twice a year - in September and on the Sunday preceding the first Sunday of May - on the occasion of the renewal of the prodigy of the liquefaction, are kept instead in the 17th-century **Cappella del Tesoro di S. Gennaro**, which are full of frescoes and decorations. In the **Sacristy**, together with 44 silver busts of the joint patron saints of Naples, we can admire instead the splendid *reliquary bust of S. Gennaro*, a true masterpiece of the goldsmith's art executed in the 14th century by the French masters Étienne Godefroyd, Guillaume de Verdelay and Milet d'Auxerre.

In the monumental interior of the Duomo a splendid chapel with lavish decoration houses the Treasure of S. Gennaro. Among the most precious relics are the bust of the saint and two phials containing the martyr's blood.

The Museo Archeologico Nazionale, housing a wealth of priceless treasures. Among the works it houses are the Jupiter of the Capitoline Triad of Cumae, a delightful Nereid and a lively fresco from Stabia representing Spring.

MUSEO ARCHEOLOGICO NAZIONALE. Outstanding masterpieces, though of a quite different kind, are also conserved in the extremely rich **Museo Archeologico Nazionale**, one of the most important in the world for the quantity and quality of the Hellenistic and Roman finds in its collections. The museum is housed in a palace that was built in 1585 as the Cavalry Barracks and later transformed into the seat of the University. The museum was created in it on the wishes of Charles of Bourbon, who considered this building to be the most suitable for housing the splendid Farnese Collection, which was acquired by the king as his maternal inheritance and which was supplemented by a great number of interesting objects coming from the excavations of Pompeii and Herculaneum. Today the museum boasts an incomparable wealth of statues, bronzes, paintings, frescoes, mosaics, architectural finds, reliefs, cameos and ceramics of Pompeian, Campanian, Apulian, Lucanian, Attic and Etruscan provenance, and offers an unrivalled panorama of centuries of classical history and culture. The Biblioteca Nazionale also had its seat in its rooms until 1922, the year in which it was transferred to the Palazzo Reale.

The monumental complex of Castel S. Elmo, which includes the splendid Certosa di S. Martino.

CASTEL S. ELMO. Worthy of particular attention is the monumental complex which stands on the hill where today the Vomero has developed and consists of **Castel S. Elmo** and the **Certosa di S. Martino**. The former was built by order of Robert I of Anjou between 1329 and 1343 and, by reason of the tufaceous stone with which it was built, the ramparts and communication trenches as well as the architectural structure, is clearly reminiscent of the nearby Castel dell'Ovo. Built to defend Naples from invasions from the sea - the fortress witnessed numerous sieges and repeated popular uprisings - it was later converted into a prison and during the Second World War risked being destroyed by the Germans. Today it is used to house interesting historico-artistic exhibitions, but is noted also for the fine **church of S. Elmo** and for the 17th-century **chapel of S. Maria del Pilar**, which have always been an integral part of the whole complex.

CERTOSA DI S. MARTINO. The **Certosa di S. Martino**, standing in a panoramic position on the edge of the Vomero hill, was built in the Angevin period and finished in the second half of the 14th century at the time of Queen Joan I. Numerous architects worked on its construction, including Tino da Camaino. Several times reorganized, and renovated in the 17th century according to the canons of the most typical Neapolitan Baroque, the Certosa is composed of a splendid **church** with a single nave, splendidly frescoed and decorated, of a **Great Cloister** and of the so-called **Cloister of the Procurators**, both of 16th-century workmanship. In its interior is the **Museo Nazionale di S. Martino** which offers an interesting section on the history and art of the city between the 17th and 19th centuries.

MUSEI DI CAPODIMONTE. Another extremely important institution, the **Museo** and **Gallerie Nazionali di Capodimonte**, a true treasure casket of precious works or art, is housed in the impressive **Palazzo Reale di Capodimonte**, created, in the intentions of Charles of Bourbon, as a hunting lodge and transformed into a harmonious and grandiose royal residence on designs by Antonio Medrano. The works, begun in 1738, required more than a century to be finally completed, thanks also to the decisive

Neapolitan masks of
past and present:
Pulcinella and Totò.

NEAPOLITAN MASKS

Pulcinella - a typical Neapolitan mask originally from the Commedia dell'Arte and according to tradition created in the 16th century by Silvio Fiorillo - in the old days wore the costume of the inhabitants of the surrounding Neapolitan countryside, to which grotesque elements like the hunchback and the hooked pimply nose were later added. Rapidly spreading to France and England, over the centuries the mask had some illustrious interpreters, like the Cammarano family, the three Petito and, in the 20th century, Ettore Petrolini and Eduardo de Filippo. The latter's brother, Peppino, together with Antonio de Curtis, the unforgettable Totò - whose own assymetrical face and jerky movements became the identifying features of an unmistakable character - can be considered as modern Neapolitan masks which have retained the light-headed, farcical character and impish resourcefulness of the old Pulcinella.

contribution of Ferdinando Fuga, who from 1764 took charge of the project. Around the splendid residence extends a vast **park** full of centuries-old trees, abundantly populated in the past by wild game. Here also is the 18th-century building housing the celebrated **Manifattura di Porcellane di Capodimonte**.

MODERN NAPLES. Paradoxically favoured by the heavy destruction suffered during the last War, the development of modern Naples has proved to be both authoritative and prolific. The expansion of the city has finished by incorporating the delightful belt of hills that has always crowned the settlement of the plain. The **Vomero**, **Posillipo Alto** and **Arenella**, which can also be reached by means of funicular railways, are thus noteworthy as pleasant residential areas, while lower down the **harbour**, fitted out with modern equipment, is today one of the main tourist and mercantile ports of call in the Mediterranean.

By now the pizza is well-known all over the world, even being appreciated even at the White House in Washington.

PIZZA

I t would be no exageration to say that the pizza is a true symbol of Italy throughout the world. And yet, in conquering the Old and above all the New Continent this flat loaf, with its name of uncertain etymology, traces its origins to Naples itself, after having enthused commonfolk and sovereigns alike, despite its essentially 'poor' nature. Made of bread dough, and garnished with oil, it is flavoured with oregano and covered with tomatoes, to which mozzarella cheese and anchovies are added, and then baked in the oven. In time the multiplication of ingredients has given rise to dozens of varieties, which flourish today in innumerable pizza restaurants. Despite this, the irreplaceable 'Napoletana' and 'Margherita' are undoubtedly the 'classics'.

Modern Naples: the S. Paolo Stadium and below, the harbour.

VESUVIUS

The ease of access, the proximity of a large urban centre and, above all, its own tormented history, have always attracted to Vesuvius, the only active volcano in continental Europe, the attention of scholars, historians and even artists who have been lured by its sombre charm. The volcano is in fact composed of two reliefs, **Monte Somma** (1132 m), a 25,000 year-old semicircular ridge, and **Vesuvius** proper (1281 m), which is situated inside the enclosure of Mount Somma in an off-centre position, shifted southwards, a truncated cone with a crater in the middle. Between them stretches the **Valle dell'Inferno**, created by the subsidence of the ancient volcano of which Monte Somma is today the only relic, a subsidence that probably took place after the eruption of 79 AD which obliterated the cities of Pompeii and Herculaneum.

VESUVIUS NATIONAL PARK

The Vesuvius National Park - extending over a total area of 8482 hectares and incorporating 13 municipalities - was established in June 1995 with a twofold objective: on the one hand safeguarding the Vesuvian territory from extensive environmental aggression, consisting mainly of cement and waste, which became particularly violent after the Second World War; and on the other acquainting people with new aspects of the volcano, its wild scenery, its traditions, and its particularly rich and celebrated agriculture. The volcanic complex of Somma-Vesuvius is distinguished in

fact by an absolutely unique concentration of mineralogical species, by an extremely varied wildlife - about thirty species of mammals, about a hundred types of birds, including the barn owl, the symbol of the park, and about a dozen reptile and amphibian species - and by its flora, grouped into various climatic belts, so rich, beyond the plants most commonly associated with Vesuvius - broom and orchid - as to have made this the most intensely studied volcano by botanists of recent centuries.

Examples of the extraordinary variety of animals and plants characterizing the Vesuvius area.

The phenomenon, which followed a period of dormancy that was so long as to have made people forget the volcanic nature of the mountain, was distinguished by particular violence and caused the complete emptying of the magma chamber. This disastrous eruption, masterfully described by Pliny the Younger, was followed by numerous others, some equally destructive, such as the one of 1631 which devastated all the settlements of the southern slope where volcanic material had always poured out, and the one of 1944, whose lava flow even today can be perceived in the Atrio del Cavallo. Since then Vesuvius has calmed down, but frequent seismic phenomena attest that this is merely an "active repose", one that is carefully controlled by a special observatory. In the meantime the undoubted environmental fascination of the volcanic complex attracts an increasing number of tourists. In the course of the centuries many illustrious figures have wanted to experience the thrill of venturing up its slopes: Seneca, Martial, Casanova, Goethe, Mozart, Stendhal, Shelley, Dumas and Dickens, and so on up to the contemporary Andy Warhol. But the tranquil dormancy of the volcano has also encouraged an excessive degree of urban development, with the establishment of heavily populated agglomerations even at the very foot of Vesuvius. Heedless of the eloquent signals launched by the eruption of 1944, which devastated S. Sebastiano al Vesuvio and Massa di Somma, human beings yet again seem intent on making their perennial challenge to this restless mountain.

Cloaked in bushes of broom and lined with paths traversed by excursionists and nature enthusiasts, Mount Vesuvius rises up with its great crater, now devoid of the traditional plume of smoke which turned into a dense and menacing volcanic cloud during eruptions.

POZZUOLI, BAIA, BACOLI, CAPO MISENO, CUMAE

The urban fabric of present-day Pozzuoli, with its busy fishing harbour, is still dominated by the imposing mass of the Amphitheatre.

Beyond the hill of Posillipo, where sky and sea seem to blend into a single, intense tonality of azure, extends a vast area of incomparable environmental and naturalistic value. Much of the credit for this can be attributed to its volcanic nature, which has given rise to the phenomenon of bradyseism, the slow action of the rising and sinking of land capable of creating situations that are highly suggestive to say the least. So it is that

at **Pozzuoli**, today an active agricultural, fishing, industrial and tourist centre, situated in the very heart of the Phlegraean Fields, the ancient public market - mistakenly identified, following the discovery of a statue of Serapis, as a place of cult consecrated to this god of Greek and Roman Egypt and conventionally indicated as *Serapeo* - appears partially submerged by the waters, whose level has varied repeatedly in the course of the centuries. Interesting evidence of this is provided by the date mussels, molluscs living at the surface of the water which have left traces of their presence at different levels on the stones and columns of the market, thus making possible a fairly precise reconstruction of the various historical phases of brady-

seism. Of the ancient Roman colony, built on a tufaceous promontory, which very soon became one of the most important ports of call in the entire Mediterranean, all of what was once the *harbour area*, with storehouses and the foundations of the wharf, is now submerged. On the acropolis, where the Duomo was later erected, a large *temple* of the Augustan period was built, imposing remains of which, together with those of the *Baths* and the *Stadium*, have recently been brought to light. These are flanked by the bulk of the majestic *Amphitheatre*, one of the largest in Italy, constructed at the time of Vespasian on the site of an older arena.

The so-called Serapeo, which was in fact not a place of cult, but a public market of the Roman age; and some views of the substantial, partly underground structures of the Amphitheatre.

As unequivocal evidence of the volcanic nature of the Phlegraean Fields, in the context of an extremely irregular landscape, the low hills alternate with numerous crateric depressions. One of these, near Pozzuoli, is noteworthy for its existing secondary volcanic phenomena: fumaroles, hyperthermal springs and small volcanoes of hot mud. This is the celebrated **solfatara**, which is nothing other than a volcano in a laborious phase of dormancy. Other basins, instead, contain delightful little lakes some of which are particularly evocative, like **Lago d'Averno**, which the ancients, perhaps because of the dark colour of its waters, or perhaps because of the surrounding environment, had no hesitation in designating as the entrance to the Underworld.

The undoubted resources of the area linked to its volcanic nature have

The desolate natural scenery of the solfatara, with its uninterrupted manifestations of volcanic origin, just as the crater today occupied by the Lago d'Averno is also of volcanic origin.

been highly appreciated ever since the Roman period. It is no accident that the present-day seaside resort of **Baia**, a short distance from Pozzuoli, dominated today by a 16th-century *castle*, was celebrated by the poet Horace as one of the most enchanting holiday sites in the world, renowned for the salubriousness of its climate and for its precious thermal waters, which from the Augustan period earned it the official status of imperial residence. Its prosperity, however, was severely put to the test from the 4th century AD by a long series of earthquakes and by the pro-

gressive accentuation of the phenomenon of bradyseism, which led to the slow submersion of the coast and of many Roman buildings. The final blow came in the 16th century, when a devastating earthquake practically razed the town to the ground. However, the archeological excavations undertaken in 1950 have made it possible to reconstruct the entire structure of the grandiose thermal complex, comprising the *Baths of Venus*, the *Baths of Sosandra*, the *Baths of Mercury*, the terraces and the *Lower Baths*. The so-called *Temples of Mercury, Venus and Diana*, dating from the Augustan age, are also of considerable importance, while the numerous and extremely interesting works of art discovered in the course of excavations are today in large part conserved in the Museo Nazionale in Naples.

The nearby **Bacoli**, a seaside and fishing resort, which was once a popular holiday site called Bauli, also preserves impressive vestiges of the splendours of the Roman period. Evidence of it today can be admired in the imposing remains of the *Cento Camerelle*, a complex system of cisterns belonging to a Roman villa (1st century BC or 1st century AD), and another cistern of the Augustan period carved into the tufa rock and known as the *Piscina Mirabile*.

The peninsula on which Bacoli lies, sticking out towards the Channel of Procida, culminates in the characteristic **Capo Miseno**, which encloses the Gulf of Pozzuoli to the west and which is nothing other than the last remnant of an ancient crater deeply eroded by the action of the waves. The enchanting beauty of the place inspired the ancient inhabitants to identify it as the site of the Elysian Fields. But the peculiar tumulus-like form of this stupendous cape also caused it to be identified as the legendary tomb of Misenus, who Virgil said was the son of Aeolus, first the companion of Hector and then of Aeneas, made to fall into the sea by a triton envious of his remarkable skills as a bugler and carried by the waves, by now a corpse, onto the Campanian beach, where he is supposed to have been buried.

Following the coastline of the delightful promontory of **Monte di Miseno**, where the Romans built splendid villas and where today we encounter the characteristic settlement of **Monte di Procida**, rising in a

Views of the Temple of Apollo and the paving-stones of the Via Sacra in the archeological area of Cumae.

Two views of the Temple of Jupiter, at Cumae, with the baptismal basin, and the long corridor with a trapezoidal section known as the Cave of the Cumaean Sibyl, where the celebrated prophetess entrusted to the wind her responses written on leaves.

An aerial view of Baia, where the characteristic Temple of Venus is located. Below, the elegant Royal Villa built by Vanvitelli on the Lago Fusaro.

The archeological area of Baia revolves around the imposing vestiges of an ancient imperial Palatium, and still houses the remains of numerous rooms used as baths, like the great Theatre-Nymphaeum with its circular basin. Not far from here is the delightful promontory of Bacoli, with the unmistakable form of Capo Miseno at its tip, and across the sea the characteristic profile of the island of Capri. Threatening and at the same time protective stands the massive castle of Baia on the same sea.

Bacoli is distinguished by the extreme richness of its archeological area, where interesting structures, like the celebrated Piscina Mirabile, have been brought to light. Also noteworthy the unmistakable shape of the extreme tip of Capo Miseno, an ancient volcanic crater modelled by the incessant erosion of the sea.

panoramic position in front of the homonymous island, beyond **Lago Fusaro**, to the north, we reach a locality of undoubted archeological interest, **Cumae**. Probably founded by the Chalcidians of Euboea in the 8th century BC in an area distinguished by particularly fertile terrain, Cumae developed rapidly, quickly acquiring total hegemony over a good part of the coasts of Campania, a hegemony that enabled it to victoriously resist the rampant expansion of the Etruscans. Conquered by the Samnites, it later passed, in 338 BC, under the control of the Romans, of whom it would always show itself to be an absolutely trustworthy ally. In spite of this, its importance inevitably diminished with the rising fortunes

of Naples, Baia and Pozzuoli, which contributed to its progressive and inexorable decline. Even today, however, we can admire the grandeur of the ancient settlement in the surviving stretches of walls that once surrounded the acropolis and in the remains of the *Temple of Apollo* and another even larger religious building. Conquered by the Goths, who barricaded themselves here in 560, resisting the siege of the troops of Narsete, in 1216 the city was completely destroyed by the Neapolitans. Later it made a comeback, though with diminished ambitions. Today, next to the archeological site, and distinguished by the same name, we find a small busy modern town immersed in a gentle landscape of enchanting beauty.

HERCULANEUM

In the course of the 1st century AD the coastal zone south-east of Naples was struck by devastating natural phenomena: first an earthquake, which on 5 February 63 AD seriously damaged the buildings of many towns; then, on 24 August 79 AD, the sudden and unexpected awakening of Vesuvius which erupted violently and literally obliterated every form of life from the slopes of the mountain.

On these slopes lay the peaceful town of **Herculaneum**, whose population at the time of the catastrophe numbered 5000. Founded, according to legend, by Heracles on his return voyage from Iberia - a myth that would seem to confirm its probable Greek origin - Herculaneum belonged successively to the Oscans, the Etruscans, the Pelasgians, the Samnites and finally the Romans, who, after the destruction inflicted upon them by the troops of a legate of Silla in 89 BC, granted them first the status of municipium and then that of colony. From then on Herculaneum enjoyed a rapid development and transformed itself into a charming residential town favoured by wealthy Roman patricians as a holiday resort; many splendid villas; an extremely regular network of streets based on

The aerial view shows up the extremely regular layout of Herculaneum, with its streets cossing at rightangles, and the admirable state of conservation of the buildings. In the background the town of Resina, whose presence has prevented the total recovery of the buried city.

Three of the most interesting buildings brought to light at Herculaneum. Above, the Baths of the Forum, the city's main complex, divided into male and female sections whose interiors are richly decorated, generally with mosaics inevitably representing sea scenes. Below, the splendid Samnite House, celebrated for the Tuscan atrium with an impluvium and a false upper storey consisting of an open gallery with closed intercolumns; light comes in through a small square opening in the ceiling embellished with an artistic frieze bearing reliefs. On the opposite page the splendour of the so-called House of Neptune and Amphitrite, which takes its name from a splendid mosaic adorning a wall of the nymphaeum.

an octagonal groundplan, with roads crossing precisely at rightangles; and large *insulae* several stories high reserved for the native population, which was engaged above all in fishing activities with only a fairly limited development of commercial activities. In 79 AD a flow of volcanic materials and mud carried by the torrential rains following the eruption of Vesuvius buried all this, penetrating into the most remote corners and forcing the population to flee. The mud, which accumulated to a height of between 12 and 30 metres, gradually solidified into a single compact block, covering the city completely and preserving it practically intact, including its perishable content, thus making possible, at a distance of almost two thousand years, the restitution of wooden structures, fabrics, ornaments and even documents.

The 18th-century discovery of Herculaneum happened almost by chance. In 1709 a farmer, digging a well, found ancient marbles which he sold to a marbleworker. The sight of them prompted Prince d'Elbeuf, commander of the Austrian contingent in Naples, to start the first, relatively limited,

The House of the Stags is certainly one of the richest houses in Herculaneum. With its inner garden and stupendous decorations, it has yielded a veritable patrimony of art works, including the celebrated marble statues of the "Drunken Hercules" and the "Satyr with a wineskin".

'personal' campaign of excavation. However, both he, and for that matter the Bourbons who sponsored the successive and much more thorough archeological campaign, were intent not so much on bringing the city back to light, as on recovering the precious finds, the statues and the buried treasures. To break into the very hard layer which preserved them numerous underground tunnels were dug, which were later filled in again with the same unearthed material, but which finished by weakening the structures of the buried buildings, complicating in no small measure the archeological campaigns which from the 19th century were launched to bring the entire city back to light. Even today the excavations are partial, inevitably impeded by the presence of the modern town of Resina, which stands on top of a vast section of the buried city and whose inhabitants have several times expressed their fear that the town might be endangered by the carrying out of exacavation campaigns.

Thus, a large part of the area of the Forum remains unexplored, while the existing remains of public building are far from numerous. What has been discovered, however, is the *Theatre*, the *Basilica* and the great Julio-Claudian *Baths*, strictly divided into two sections, male and female, with separate entrances. The roads have a paving dating from the Augustan period, are flanked by sidewalks and are only slightly worn down by the passage of carts, thus confirming the existence of a fairly limited commercial traffic, which was probably effected with the use of porters. The almost total absence of a sewerage system - the waste from the houses, excluding the outlets of the latrines, provided with wells, opened directly on to the road - was counterbalanced by the presence of an aqueduct which supplied the entire city.

Many buildings have produced valuable evidence of daily life, but also of an impressive artistic production (paintings, sculptures, mosaics). So it is for the *House of Argus*, only partially brought to light; for the *House of the Wooden Screen*, with its spacious Tuscan atrium; for the *House of the Mosaic Atrium*, standing in a panoramic position and divided into two distinct parts, which takes its name from the fine pavements of the vestibule and atrium; for the *Samnite House*, with its splendid Tuscan atrium; for the *House of Neptune and Amphitrite*, represented in a glass mosaic on a wall of the highly decorated nymphaeum; for the *House of the Bicentenary*, excavated in 1938, the second centenary of the official opening of systematic excavations at Herculaneum, and possibly inhabited by a family that practised the cult of Christianity, as we are led to believe by a cross carved into the plaster of one room under which a wooden altar or prie-dieu was discovered; for the elegant *House of the Stags*, which contained valuable marble statues - including the "Deer attacked by dogs" and the celebrated "Drunken Hercules"; and for the *House of the*

Built on several levels, the House of the Telephos Relief is one of the largest houses in the city, with an elegant atrium whose columns, painted red like the walls, support the architrave of the upper floor. The name of the house derives from a relief of neo-Attic art in which the myth of Telephos was represented.

Telephos Relief. Also noteworthy is the monumental *Palaestra*, which occupies an entire *insula*, the *Suburban Baths* and the lavish and panoramic *Villa of the Papyruses* or *of the Pisoni*, this also suburban, which has, among its precious treasures, produced some 200 papyruses for the most part philosophical in content. This comes as no surprise since one of its owners was Lucius Calpurnius Pisone Caesoninus, the father-in-law of Julius Caesar and protector among others of the Epicurean philosopher Philodemus of Gadara. Included among the marble and bronze sculptures which embellished the building, today conserved at the Museo Nazionale in Naples, is the herma of Doriphorus of Polycletus.

Both the *Palaestra* and the *Suburban Baths* must have had much greater importance in the context of city life. The former, provided with a monumental columned entrance and a swimming pool situated in the middle of an uncovered area surrounded by an arcade, was reserved for athletic activities and consisted of an open gallery for the public and an apsed hall used for prize-givings. The latter, divided up as was customary into "frigidarium", "calidarium" and "tepidarium" but not into male and female sections, did not look particularly imposing from the outside, but inside they should be noted for the decorations and for the refinement of the details, like the marble herma of Apollo that spouts water into the basin of the vestibule.

VESUVIAN OBSERVATORY

The restless mountain of Vesuvius, capable of violent eruptions and long periods of dormancy, undoubtedly requires careful monitoring. With this in mind, between 1841 and 1845 the Vesuvian Observatory was instituted on the Neapolitan side of the volcano, at an altitude of 608 m, equipped with a well-stocked specialized library and a small museum. Today its instruments are the most reliable means of assessing the unpredictable activity of the volcano.

Three different images of Herculaneum: the large House of Argus, with its peristyle surrounding the spacious garden on three sides; the Palaestra, with its long portico flanked by Corinthian columns; and the simple facade of the Suburban Baths, which curiously enough lacked the usual division into male and female sections.

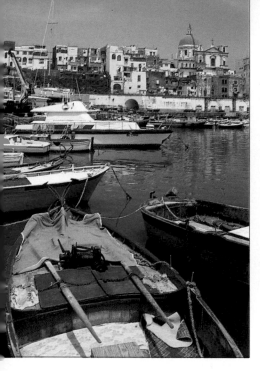

Present-day Torre Annunziata is an industrious seaside town with a busy port. But its remote past is that of a splendid residential centre where elegant Roman villas flourished.

TORRE DEL GRECO
AND TORRE ANNUNZIATA

Proceeding along the coast we come to **Torre del Greco**, this too lying at the foot of Vesuvius. From here it is possible to reach the *Vesuvian Observatory* and then, with a chair-lift, the summit of the crater. Known in antiquity as Turris Octava because its tower was the eighth that stood on the coast between Naples and Castellammare, and then by its present name, which may refer to the "Greek" wine produced in the area, the town is world-famous not only for fishing and coral-working, for shells and mother-of-pearl, but also for the working of ivory, lava, and semi-precious stones. To the art of carving, particularly coral, a museum and school, founded as long ago as 1878, have been dedicated.

The name of the nearby **Torre Annunziata** is also linked to another guard-tower and a 14th-century chapel dedicated to Our Lady of the Annunciation. A heavily populated and active industrial and commercial

centre, as well as a popular thermal resort, the town, embellished by the churches of *S. Maria del Carmine* and *S. Maria del Suffragio*, as well as by the *sanctuary of Madonna della Neve*, may be seen as the modern heir of the ancient **Oplonti**. The latter was probably not a real city, but rather an elegant residential centre. Splendid evidence for this are the monumental villas which excavations have brought to light ever since the 18th century. Situated in a splendid bay, they comprised the noble periphery of Pompeii. Among the other villas we should note the magnificent residence belonging to Poppaea, the wife of the emperor Nero: consisting of over 90 rooms, with gardens, baths and an enormous swimming pool, it was decorated by statues and wall paintings representing architecture and landscapes. When the eruption of Vesuvius buried it, it was probably uninhabited and undergoing restoration.

The Villa of Poppaea, in ancient Oplonti, still preserves intact the beauty of its rooms and their decorations, which consist mainly of naturalistic subjects.

POMPEII, THE BURIED CITY

A crueller fate, in the tragedy of 79 AD, undoubtedly involved **Pompeii**. This city was buried under a rain of ash and small volcanic stones which in just 30 hours had accumulated to a height of 7 metres, and before this was enveloped by an enormous cloud of poisonous gases, that same pine-shaped cloud described by Pliny the Younger. For most of the 30,000 inhabitants of the city there was no escape. Today, striking evidence of the dramatic unfolding of the disaster is revealed in the numerous plaster casts of those who, instead of seeking salvation by fleeing towards the sea, took shelter in their homes, in their storerooms and under the arcades, where they met their death. And as proof of the unexpectedness of the event, the excavations - begun scientifically in 1748 under the reign of Charles of Bourbon - after various, occasional discoveries of ancient finds brought to light an entire city in which daily life seemed suddenly to have stopped: dead dogs still chained, beasts of burden tied up, bread and other food just taken out of

the ovens, just as on any other ordinary day.

In the 1st century AD, Pompeii was a prosperous commercial town lying in the fertile basin of the Sarno river, endowed with a well-equipped and well-visited port. Of ancient Osco-Campanian origin, until the 5th century BC the settlement had been maintained within the sphere of influence of the Etruscans, who were stationed at Capua, and later of the Greeks, who had one of their most flourishing colonies at Cumae. Many elements, in the buildings and more in general in Pompeian artistic expression, still provide incontrovertible proof of this. In the course of the 5th century the Samnites took possession of the whole Agro Campano and for Pompeii a period of urban expansion began. At the beginning of the 3rd century, having passed under Roman domination, the city, now surrounded by imposing walls, drew enormous benefit from the expansion of Roman influence over the Mediterranean and from the consequent intensification of commercial traffic. The florid economic condition, to which not even the substantial exportation of local wine and oil remained extraneous, soon

The archeological excavations have brought to light an entire city situated at the foot of the menacing bulk of Vesuvius, side to side with the modern settlement of the same name. Also brought to light, immortalized by the intense expressiveness of the famous plaster casts, is terrible evidence of the human drama experienced by those who failed to survive the tragic eruption of 79 AD.

Two of the most important religious buildings in Pompeii were the Temple of Apollo, introduced by the celebrated statue of the god, of which the liturgical area and the altar are still clearly recognizable, and the Temple of Jupiter, situated between two triumphal arches. The grandiose Amphitheatre and the Great Theatre, flanked by the Odeion, were reserved instead for performances of a quite different kind.

Around the vast square of the large Civic Forum the social, economic, legal and more simply daily life of the city revolved. Here business deals were concluded, politics was discussed, and justice was administered. The grandiose Basilica represented the place destined for this latter activity and for the definition of the city's most important social and economic affairs.

The Basilica must have appeared this austere and monumental to the inhabitants of Pompeii in the 1st century AD.

favoured the rapid development of sumptuous public and private building. The siege of Silla's troops in 89 BC and the successive conversion of the settlement into a colony with the name of Colonia Veneria Cornelia Pompeianorum did nothing to alter the town's prosperity, which on the contrary found concrete new incentives in the conspicuous influx of well-to-do philo-Augustan families who turned Pompeii into a pleasant residential centre. Not even the disastrous earthquake of 63 AD succeeded in subduing the city: numerous buildings were seriously damaged, but there was an immediate determination to restore them to their earlier splendour. Promptly undertaken, the work of restoration work was long and complex, to the point that a large part of it could hardly be considered finished when the destructive fury of Vesuvius wreaked devastation upon the city.

As was customary in the Roman urban and administrative system, the life of Pompeii revolved around

Two of the buildings overlooking the Forum are worth a special mention: the Temple of Jupiter, the main religious structure in the city, and the Building of Eumachia, notable for its imposing sacredness.

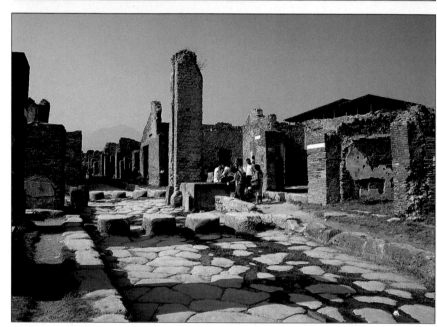

Two of the city's main roads, the Via Stabiana and the Via dell'Abbondanza, whose name derived from the erroneous identification of the mask on a fountain which actually represented the Concordia Augusta.

the *Civic Forum*, the true heart of the city, a vast rectangular area originally flanked by arcades. Giving onto the forum was the majestic *Basilica* (2nd century BC), divided into three naves, the place used for the administration of justice but also for the definition of the most important economic and social affairs; the *Temple of Apollo* (2nd century BC), inspired by Hellenistic architectural models and seriously damaged by the earthquake of 63 AD; the *Forum Holitorium*, a large open arcade used to house the storerooms and the market for the sale of cereals; the *Temple of Jupiter*, the main religious building in the city, in reality dedicated to the Capitoline Triad of Jupiter, Juno and Minerva, flanked by two *triumphal arches*, the western one dedicated to Drusus and the eastern one either to Tiberius or to Germanicus; the *Macellum*, the food market of Pompeii; the *Sanctuary of the Lares*, built after the earthquake of 63 AD to win the favour of the tutelary deities; the *Temple of Vespasian*, with its small irregular plan, dedicated to the cult of the emperor and not yet brought to completion at the time of the eruption; the splendid *Building of Eumachia*, named after the priestess of Venus who had it built in the Tiberian age and used to house the corporations of the manufacturers, launderers and dyers of woollen cloth; its facade, preceded by a portico with two or

ders of columns, on whose architrave an inscription informs that the building was dedicated to the Concordia Augusta and to the Pietas, was certainly rebuilt in brick after having been damaged by the earthquake.
From the Forum departed the long, rectilinear Via dell'Abbondanza, one of the *decumani* of the city - that is, one of the streets traversing the entire town in an east-west direction - which gets its name from a fountain with a basin bearing the representation of the Concordia Augusta, mistakenly identified as the personification of Abundance. Measuring 8.5 metres across at its widest, and probably repaved in the last years of the town's existence, the street ran alongside the monumental *Stabian Baths*. These were equipped with a palaestra and a swimming pool and were decorated with polychrome stuccoes not unlike those embellishing another thermal establishment in the city, erected in 80 BC in the area of the Forum, behind the Temple of Jupiter. Proceeding along the Via dell'Abbondanza we come across a characteristic line of shops, which it seems were multiplied as part of the reconstruction work after the earthquake. Only along the furthest and most outlying stretch of the street are there more private homes, like the *House of Octavius Quartius* and that of *Julia Felix*, whose size, ground-plan and the presence of an ample and well-tended garden can be readily compared with the large suburban villas.
The Via dell'Abbondanza ends at the *Porta a Sarno*, one of the seven gates inserted in the city's perimeter walls, together with *Porta Nola*, *Por-*

Overlooking the Via dell'Abbondanza were the grandiose and extremely well-frequented Stabian Baths, equipped with a palaestra, and the splendid House of Octavius Quartius, lavishly decorated with frescoes and in many ways very similar to one of the elegant suburban mansions typical of Roman urban centres.

If the Temple of Isis, with its distinctive ground-plan - note the cella which is wider than it is long - is interesting evidence of the diffusion reached by this cult of Egyptian origin in the 1st century AD, the elegant House of the Faun is famous not so much for the small bronze that gave it its name, but particularly for the splendid mosaics, including the one representing tragic masks amid festoons.

ta Vesuvio, *Porta Ercolano, Porta Marina, Porta Stabia* and *Porta Nocera*. This is the area occupied by the *Great Palaestra* and the majestic *Amphitheatre*. The latter, built in 80 BC and capable of holding 12,000 spectators, was used for gladiatorial contests and in 59 AD was the scene of a bloody riot between the Pompeians and Nucerians.

South of the Via dell'Abbondanza we find the area of the theatres, flanked by the *Triangular Forum*, which is closed on three sides by an arcade with 95 Doric columns while the south-west side was left free to avoid blocking the magnificent panoramic view towards the sea. In the middle of the Forum stood an ancient *Doric Temple* (6th century BC), which was modified several times and of which nothing survives today other than the base. Joined to this temple, as evidence of a common sacred value, is the *Great Theatre*, which betrays its Hellenistic origin (3rd-

The sumptuous House of the Vettii is particularly interesting for the lavish and highly refined wall decorations consisting of splendid frescoes with architectural and mythological subjects.

2nd century BC) in the horse-shoe shaped orchestra and in the cavea, obtained by exploiting the natural gradient of a slope without the support of any masonry structure, and capable of holding 5000 spectators, more than three times the number that could enter the adjacent *Odeion*, or *Small Theatre*. Built in 80 BC, this building was used for spectacles such as mime and musical recitals which required a smaller auditorium. According to Greek tradition, in the immediate vicinity of the Theatre there was always a spacious arcade, which gave spectators the opportunity to entertain themselves during the intervals. The Great Theatre of Pompeii also had one, with 74 Doric columns. However, after the earthquake it was appropriately modified and turned into a barracks for the gladiators. A stairway gives access instead to the nearby *Temple of Isis*, erected in the 2nd century BC and after the devastation of the earthquake magnificently restored by Numerius Popidius Ampliatus, a well-to-do freedman. Its existence, and the richness of the offerings that have been found in it, today provide important evidence of the extent of the diffusion of this cult imported from Egypt into the Roman world.

The magnificence of life at Pompeii was also reflected in the splendour of private homes. We should mention, for example, the *House of the Faun*, situated not far from the great *Central Baths* and the *Temple of Fortuna Augusta*, the latter commissioned by Marcus Tullius, a private citizen called, at the time of Augustus, to hold the most important public offices. Severely damaged by the earthquake, when the eruption of Vesuvius buried the temple it had not yet been completely restored. The House of the Faun gets its name from a small bronze statue that

embellished the atrium, although it is also distinguished by a great many other splendid features: its remarkable size, primarily, being organized, in practice, into two quarters that occupied an entire block; and, among its other merits, certainly the elegance of the mosaics that decorated it, including the very famous one representing the military conflict between Alexander the Great and Darius, today housed at the Museo Nazionale in Naples. Another large and sumptuous residence must have been the *House of the Vettii*, elegantly rebuilt in the course of the 1st century AD by the owners, two freedmen who had become rich, a symbol of the rapid economic rise of the mercantile classes. The wall decorations are particularly fine, comprising elaborate cycles of frescoes with mythological subjects. But there were of course numerous private dwellings worthy of the greatest interest: the *House of Menandrus*, the *House of the Diadumeni*, the *House of Marcus Lucretius*, the *House of the Golden Cupids*, the *House of the Tragic Poet*, known, besides its frescoes, for the original mosaic with the inscription "Beware of the Dog" (in Latin "Cave canem") which stands out significantly on the pavement of the entrance. Also worth mentioning is the *Suburban Villa*, dating from the imperial age, standing immediately outside the Porta Marina, against the walls, and ornamented

with elaborate decorations; and above all the *Villa of the Mysteries*, this too suburban, datable to the 2nd century BC and certainly restructured several times. Among its most important fresco cycles, some distinguished by bold architectural perspective, the decoration of the salon is particularly striking, one of the most celebrated paintings of the ancient world: enormous in size (17 x 3 m) and with life-sized human figures, it is entirely dedicated to the Dionysiac Mysteries and was executed between 70 and 60 BC by a Campanian painter clearly influenced by Hellenistic models. His masterpiece has succeeded in surviving in time even the violence of Vesuvius.

In recent times the archeological excavations, where the work of unearthing and recovering buildings and finds continues even today, represent a great attraction for both tourists and scholars. But in modern Pompeii, which has grown up at the southern foot of Vesuvius, there is another quite different pole of attraction that draws to it the faithful and devoted: this is the *Sanctuary of the Madonna del Rosario*, founded on 8 May 1876 by the lawyer and fervent Catholic, Bartolo Longo, completed in 1891, enlarged in 1933 and 1939 and associated with a vast network of public assistance services. The image of the Madonna preserved there is the object of great popular devotion.

CAPRI

Capri is the southernmost island in the Gulf of Naples, almost the extreme spur of the Sorrento Peninsula, from which it is separated by a short stretch of sea. Although the current view is that in antiquity the Teleboi lived here, mentioned by Virgil in the "Aeneid", there is no historical evidence for this. Instead it has been historically proved that this small island (the perimeter measures barely 17 km), with its distinctive "compressed" shape, has been inhabited by humans since prehistoric times. And when Octavian, the Roman emperor who took the name of Augustus, rediscoved its enchanting beauty at the dawn of our own era, it became one of the favourite imperial residences. Here there are supposed to be 12 imperial villas and the Augustan excavations themselves brought to light precious finds from the prehistoric and Greek periods. Augustus's successor, Tiberius, lived on the island for 10 years, from 27 to 37 AD, and many patricians of the period wanted to build their own homes here. At the fall of the Roman Empire a long period of oblivion and decline ensued, accentuat-

The 'Faraglioni', the rocks, a splendid sea, and villages immersed in unspoilt natural surroundings: this is the charm of Capri which has proved irresistible for artists and writers, like Curzio Malaparte, who stayed for a long time in the Red House.

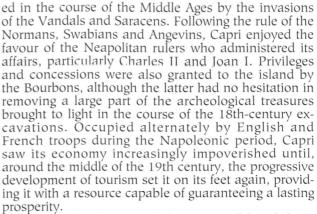

ed in the course of the Middle Ages by the invasions of the Vandals and Saracens. Following the rule of the Normans, Swabians and Angevins, Capri enjoyed the favour of the Neapolitan rulers who administered its affairs, particularly Charles II and Joan I. Privileges and concessions were also granted to the island by the Bourbons, although the latter had no hesitation in removing a large part of the archeological treasures brought to light in the course of the 18th-century excavations. Occupied alternately by English and French troops during the Napoleonic period, Capri saw its economy increasingly impoverished until, around the middle of the 19th century, the progressive development of tourism set it on its feet again, providing it with a resource capable of guaranteeing a lasting prosperity.

Today the island is one of the most well-loved destinations for artists, intellectuals, writers and more generally tourists coming from all parts of the world. Visitors are attracted by its absolutely unique charm: with a rich and extremely lush Mediterranean vegetation, although totally lacking in freshwater springs, Capri is composed of limestone rock which in the course of the centuries has tak-

Roman columns, one of which stands on the wharf of Marina Grande, and Tiberius's Drop, a precipice of savage beauty associated with sinister and dramatic legends, bear witness to a past of great splendour. The small harbour of Marina Grande instead is the image of an active and prosperous present.

en on a variety of suggestive forms, including reliefs, hills, plateaus, promontories and above all small bays, inlets, rocks and a multitude of splendid grottos.

Visitors arriving on the island land at **Marina Grande**, a well-equipped tourist resort with a splendid church, *S. Costanzo*, and in the immediate vicinity the remains of the *Palazzo a Mare di Augusto* and the adjacent *Baths of Tiberius*.

From here, either with the panoramic funicular or on foot along the steps of Via S. Francesco, one ascends to the town of **Capri**, which lies between Punta del Capo and Monte Solaro (the highest peak on the island at 589 m), surrounded by villas, gardens and citrus orchards. Built inland as a refuge from Saracen attacks, the town still has a clear medieval layout that revolves around the celebrated *Piazzetta* (Piazza Umberto I). The characteristic small domed houses, with arches and porticoes, which either look onto it or converge on it along narrow winding alleys, often incorporate the remains of ancient walls, while the 14th-century *Palazzo Cerio*, today the seat of a library and an exhibition of fossils, was in an-

The celebrated and perennially crowded Piazzetta is the true heart of Capri. But among the attractions of the island we should also mention the splendid Certosa di S. Giacomo and the unmistakable sea against the background of the Campanian coast.

tiquity the castle of Queen Joan I. Also worthy of note are the *Town Hall* and the *Clock Tower*, while a stairway leads to the 17th-century Baroque *church of S. Stefano*, which houses a silver statue of the island's patron saint, S. Costanzo.

Not far from the town centre, the *Certosa di S. Giacomo*, with an adjoining church of the same name, conserves unaltered traces of the 14th-century complex, despite subsequent modifications. Near the Certosa is a large *park*, wanted by the German industrialist F. A. Krupp and better known as the 'Gardens of Augustus'. From the terrace, immersed in vegetation, the view embraces Capri, the bay of Marina Piccola and above all the majestic *Faraglioni*, the real symbol of the island, three tall pinnacles which rise to a height of 100 m and which the sea, with the incessant,

The imposing and suggestive remains of Villa Jovis, an impressive view of the Via Krupp with its narrow hairpin bends, and a characteristic landing-stage on the southern coast of the island.

The measured elegance, the artistic and decorative richness, the distinctive harmony of the interiors and the luxurious gardens make Villa S. Michele a place of incomparable beauty.

ILLUSTRIOUS GUESTS

The fortunes of Capri have certainly known no bounds, either geographical or temporal. The emperors Augustus and Tiberius made the island their golden refuge and left lasting reminders of their presence here, even in place-names: Tiberius's Drop, the frightening abyss 300 m high above the sea, which according to the historian Tacitus the emperor used for capital executions; the Baths of Tiberius, which were formerly of Augustus, much more peacefully overlooking the sea. No less important, almost two thousand years later, the Swedish resident Axel Munthe, esteemed court physician in Stockholm, who from 1896 had a magnificent residence, Villa S. Michele, built near Anacapri. Here he spent long periods of his life and composed his literary masterpiece, "The History of S. Michele". But Capri's illustrious guests are of course too numerous to mention: from Ferdinand Gregorovius and Alexandre Dumas to Maxim Gorki and Curzio Malaparte, literary figures and intellectuals have always shown themselves particularly receptive to the unrivalled charm of the island.

A rare photograph of Axel Munthe.

centuries-old action of its waves, has eroded into unusual shapes.
In this enchanting area, in the 1st century AD, Tiberius had his villa built, *Villa Jovis*, whose remains even today arouse the admiration of visitors. Situated in a commanding position on the far east of the island, protected by a look-out post that was later transformed into a lighthouse, this imposing construction is arranged on four storeys and can boast a total surface area of over 6000 m². The northern section of the complex housed the imperial apartments proper, graced by an airy portico, while the reception rooms were situated in the east, the servants were housed in the west wing, and to the south were the baths. The water supply for the whole complex was provided by a gigantic system of cisterns and storage reservoirs into which rainwater was channelled. Even today the grandeur of the structure, divided into enormous rooms with superb architecture, is astonishing. Not far from the villa, a precipice is known as

The delightful church of S. Michele at Anacapri, full of works of art, including the superb maiolica pavement with the representation of various biblical allegories. Below, the magical atmosphere of the Grotta Azzurra. On the opposite page, views of the attractive little island of Procida, dominated by its imposing castle.

'Tiberius's Drop'. Legend has it that the emperor had his enemies thrown over the cliffs here. What is certain is that some of his later successors, including Commodus, had the most unwanted individuals confined at Capri.

Leaving the villa, we proceed along the splendid *Via Krupp*, which is named after the German industrialist who had it built and which leads, after a series of narrow and suggestive hairpin bends high above the sea, to **Marina Piccola** and to its large bay, dominated by the Rock of the Sirens. Just above Marina Piccola is the *Grotta delle Felci*, where precious finds dating from the Stone and Bronze Ages have been found. From here the road climbs to **Anacapri**, the second largest town on the island, with

Suggestive images of the ritual procession which every year winds through the streets of Procida.

WINES OF THE GULF

On the islands of the Gulf of Naples agriculture is particularly favoured by the fertility of the soil, which means that traditional fishing activities are accompanied by the cultivation of orchards and above all vineyards from which highly-prized wines are obtained. In addition to the celebrated production of Procida, it is certainly worth mentioning the "Capri", a dry white wine ideal for drinking with fish and particularly well-suited to ageing, produced on the island it is named after, together with the "Capri rosso", which goes better with roast dishes. Ischia is noteworthy for its highly-prized "Epomeo", but also for its "Ischia bianco", a white wine suitable for fish dishes, and for its fragrant "Ischia nero".

One of the celebrated vineyards of the islands in the Gulf of Naples.

its highly distinctive small white houses that are clustered together along the central Via Orlandi. The churches are noteworthy: *S. Maria di Costantinopoli*, *S. Sofia* and above all *S. Michele*, with its 18th-century maiolica pavement. Situated, as the name suggests, 'above Capri', at the foot of Monte Solaro, this village was for a long time linked to the main town on the island only by the so-called *Phoenician Steps*, which in all probability were actually the work of early Greek colonists. Proceeding along it, today, we come to *Villa S. Michele* - which takes its name from that of an earlier chapel - a splendid residence which the Swiss doctor Axel Munthe had built at the beginning of the present century in an incomparably panoramic position. Today it houses a large number of ancient finds. The park of the villa, in one of the very rare yellow tufa areas of the island, is characterized by extraordinary vegetation.

From Anacapri a cableway leads to the summit of Monte Solaro, from which there is an impressive view that ranges as far as Ponza and the mountains of Calabria in the distance, while the road runs towards *Villa Damecuta*, a monumental imperial villa with a spacious portico and a suggestive panoramic terrace that seems almost to cling to the rocky promontory.

Undoubtedly worth a visit, finally, is the celebrated **Grotta Azzurra**, which was known to the Romans and is today extremely popular with tourists. The play of refracted sunlight entering the sea water creates a magical spectacle of colours and atmosphere.

PROCIDA

Halfway between Capo Miseno and the island of Ischia lies a small island, **Procida**, of evident volcanic origin. Formed by four craters, today barely visible, its terrain is composed entirely of yellowish tufa rock. Although totally flat (its highest point is only 91 m!), it does have fairly high cliffs, whose irregular and jagged contours create a multitude of bays and inlets, where beaches and mooring-places alternate and where fishermen's houses have ended up being concentrated. This is how **Marina Corricella** and **Marina Grande**, the main port of the island, were formed. The town of **Procida** lies in the north-east, in an elevated position, dominated by the majestic castle that was later turned into a penitentiary. Not far from here, at Terra Murata, the *abbey of S. Michele* still preserves its majestic charm intact. Situated in a pleasant panoramic position, the church is embellished by an altar in polychrome marble, and by a splendid wooden ceiling decorated with a painting by Luca Giordano representing "Lucifer being driven away by S. Michele".

Battered by the incursions of the Saracens throughout the Middle Ages, for a long time Procida could claim its own feudal lords, the most celebrated of whom was Giovanni da Procida. Between 1799 and 1813 it witnessed three English occupations, of which clear traces survive to this day. The entire island is also noted for the extraordinary fertility of its soil, a characteristic that has favoured the development of agriculture: particularly renowned are the citrus orchards and the vineyards of Procida, from which a highly prized wine is produced.

The fortified Aragonese castle perched on its islet in front of Ischia Ponte.

ISCHIA

With its almost 50 square kilometres and roughly trapezoidal shape, Ischia is the largest of the Parthenopean islands. Linked genetically to the region of the Phlegraean Fields, its own volcanic nature is betrayed in the widespread presence of fumaroles and thermal springs that have been documented since antiquity (Pliny the Elder, Strabo and Statius all make specific reference to them). And if today these volcanic phenomena provide a splendid resource for tourism, thanks to the therapeutic properties of the springs and muds, exploited by numerous thermal establishments, in the past they were cause above all of widespread devastation. It comes as no surprise that many of the populations who in antiquity intended settling on the island were obliged to abandon it, forced to flee from the eruptions of its craters, a fate shared by the early Greek colonies in the

Ischia Ponte, with its fishermen's houses dominated by the cupola of the cathedral and a long history behind it, documented by interesting finds and by splendid tombstones.

6th century BC, the Syracusans in the 5th, and later the Romans, who nonetheless turned it into a highly desirable holiday-place. Interspersed with barbarian and Saracen invasions and pillaging, the violent volcanic phenomena continued until 1301, the year of the last eruption of Monte Epomeo, which with its 788 m is the highest peak on the island. From the 15th century earthquakes continued endlessly to torment the existence of Ischia's inhabitants: no less than 15 occurred in the 19th century alone, including the disastrous one at Casamicciola, which in 1883 claimed 2000 victims.

After having experienced Angevin, Aragonese and D'Avalos rule, Ischia passed to the Bourbons in 1734, to be then temporarily occupied by the

French in 1806. Today its thermal establishments, but also its high and jagged coasts which alternate with beaches, its mild dry climate, its fertile and luxuriant nature, make it a popular place for tourism and therapeutic treatment.

The main town on the island is **Ischia**, which stretches for over 3 km between **Ischia Porto** - an ancient coastal volcanic crater turned into a harbour in 1854 with the opening of a channel that provided it with access to the sea - and **Ischia Ponte**, which gets its name from the Aragonese bridge, 228 m long, built in 1438 to link the town with the small island on which the castle stands. The castle also traces its origins to the Aragonese, who made Ischia into a veritable strategic bastion defending the Gulf of Naples. The fortified complex is composed of several highly interesting buildings, like the 14th-century *cathedral*, the former *convent of the Poor Clares* with adjoining cemetery and the 18th-century *church of the Blessed Virgin*.

Three fascinating images of Lacco Ameno: the sea-front, the celebrated and highly distinctive 'fungo', and the rich Archeological Museum.

CASAMICCIOLA TERME, LACCO AMENO, FORIO, S. ANGELO, BARANO

Proceeding in a westerly direction we come to **Casamicciola Terme**, particularly renowned for its thermal springs, and then **Lacco Ameno**, which has some interesting attractions: immersed in greenery, the town has a modern church, *S. Restituta*, built over the foundations of a basilica of 1036 with an impressive crypt; an *Archeological Museum*, where visitors can admire finds coming from the nearby necropolis (8th century BC - 3rd century AD), evidence of the fact that the first settlements on the island date from fairly remote times; and the characteristic *'fungo'*, an unmistakable outcrop of tufa rock that rises from the sea just in front of the town.

Beaches, seaside resorts, elegant swimming pools and thermal springs are found all over the island. At Forio the small chiesetta del Soccorso is an example of popular religiosity and island architecture.

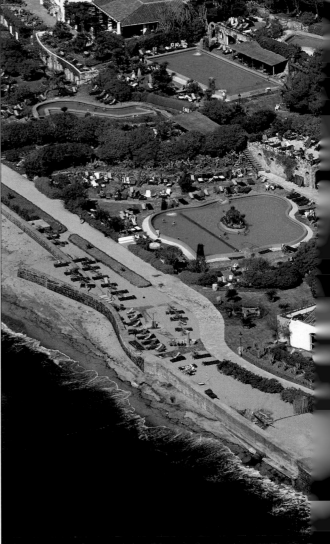

As for **Forio**, celebrated for its thermal establishments, the town can claim a small record: 12 towers had been erected to defend the town, among them the imposing *Torrione*, which rises at the side of the two maiolica bell-towers of the *church of S. Maria di Loreto*. Not far from here, on a suggestive and panoramic promontory, stands the *chiesetta del Soccorso*, where emigrants and sailors traditionally came to offer their ex-votos. Lower down lies the beautiful beach of *Citara*, in whose sea, according to the ancient Romans, the goddess Venus loved to bathe.

From here the road continues into the most impervious area of the island, characterized by cultivated terraces, tiny rural villages, high ground and hills. Here we find **S. Angelo**, an ancient fishing village dedicated to tourism, and **Barano**, clustered around the piazza of S. Rocco, with the its church that stands next to the more imposing building of the Baroque *S. Sebastiano*. And once again lots of small characteristically white houses almost clinging to the steep narrow alleys that climb up the rocky slopes.

Two images conveying all the lively charm of the enchanting village of S. Angelo d'Ischia.

CASTELLAMMARE DI STABIA

At the southernmost extremity of the Gulf of Naples, dominated by the verdant slopes of Monte Faito, from whose summit, which can be reached by cableway, visitors can admire unforgettable views, a modern town, **Castellammare di Stabia**, derives its name

from a fortified *castle* erected in the 8th century and modified in the Angevin period ("Castrum ad mare de Stabiis") and its prosperity from the presence of famous thermal establishments. In reality, the therapeutic properties of the Stabian waters were formerly appreciated by the Romans, who from an ancient Greek settlement, which had later became Etruscan and had subsequently passed to the Samnites, in the 4th century founded the flourishing colony of Stabiae. Destroyed first by Silla (89 BC), and later by Vesuvius as a result of the devastating eruption of 79 AD, the town experienced alternating fortunes both in the Middle Ages and in modern times. Today, both the *New* and the *Old Stabian Baths* are equipped with highly specialized treatment systems, although they are not the only attraction of Castellammare: the *Duomo*, built in the 16th century but restructured in the last century, houses an ancient statue of S. Michele (6th century) as well as valuable pictorial works; in the *church of Jesus* (17th century) visitors can admire the "Madonna del Soccorso", painted by Luca Gior-

Castellammare di Stabia lying along the Gulf of Naples against the background of the unmistakable form of Mount Vesuvius.

Among the town's main attractions, in addition to the large baths, is the Duomo, linked to the cult of S. Catello, and the two Roman villas brought to light by the archeological excavations together with the frescoes with which they are embellished.

dano; and the *Villa Comunale* is noteworthy for its luxuriant garden. But it is above all the *archeological excavations* of the Roman city that provide items of undoubted interest. Here two splendid patrician dwellings have been brought to light, the *Villa of Ariadne* and the *Roman Villa*, both with lavish decorations and frescoes dating from the 1st century AD. A large part of the numerous precious finds discovered in the course of excavations, including sculptures, bas-reliefs, but also objects of everyday use and funerary furnishings, are today preserved in the *Stabian Antiquarium*.

VICO EQUENSE, META, PIANO DI SORRENTO, S. AGNELLO

Proceeding along the coast from Castellammare di Stabia, we come to the Sorrento Coast, whose charming unspoilt natural scenery blends harmoniously with urban settlements of undoubted interest. A long succession of hotels, seaside resorts, gardens and citrus orchards leads to **Vico Equense**, a picturesque seaside town situated on a tufaceous bank dominated by the *castle* which Charles II of Angevin had built and which was substantially modified in the 18th century. Also interesting is the 14th-century *parish church* and the *church of SS. Ciro e Giovanni*, rebuilt in 1715. Not far away, high on the coast, lies **Meta**, which boasts the ancient *basilica della Madonna del Lauro*, but also a delightful natural setting which is undoubtedly the prime attraction of this seaside resort.
The nearby **Piano di Sorrento**, with its ancient *basilica di S. Michele*, several times modified and embellished with impressive pictorial works, also owes its prosperity to tourism, as well as to agriculture. Having

If Castellammare di Stabia can boast the Villa of Ariadne and the Roman Villa, two splendid patrician residences almost two thousand years old still decorated with elegant cycles of frescoes, Vico Equense is striking above all for the enchanting natural surroundings in which the town, with its churches and its castle, is peacefully located.

gone past **S. Agnello**, an agricultural centre surrounded by citrus orchards but above all by vineyards and olive groves that supply thriving wine-making and oil-making firms, we reach Sorrento.

The town of Sorrento, although equipped with two splendid harbours, Marina Grande and Marina Piccola, has always cultivated a curious relationship with the sea, an absolutely vital element, which it looks down upon from its tufaceous terrace.

The picturesque streets and shops of Sorrento.

SORRENTO

Sorrento is a delightful town lying on a tufaceous terrace with sheer cliffs that drop about 50 metres to sea level. Its favourable position and the climate which is rendered particularly mild by the presence, behind the city, of a ring of hills, have made it a popular holiday-place from the earliest times. Lauded by ancient and modern poets alike, from Statius to Byron, Sorrento claims remote origins: if the name is traditionally traced back to the myth of the Sirens of Ulysses (*Surrentum*), it is certain that the place was inhabited from the Neolithic period. The first real settlement, however, was the work of Greek colonists, who with the passing of time were replaced by the Etruscans, the Syracusans and the Samnites. In the 3rd century BC the Romans arrived and from then on villas, temples, gardens and baths flourished at Sorrento. Subsequently opposing the Goths, the Byzantines, the Saracens, the Amalfitans, the Normans

A striking view of the town from the harbour; Sorrento is interesting for its rich handicrafts, and, in the main square, the imposing monument to Torquato Tasso, perhaps the most celebrated product of this enchanting city.

and other more or less warlike neighbours, the city can certainly claim to have had a tormented history up until the end of the 18th century, but also proudly claims to be the birthplace of Torquato Tasso. It is precisely to the celebrated 16th-century poet, to whom a monument has also been raised, that the *main piazza* of Sorrento is dedicated, a square flanked by the well-lit *church of S. Maria del Carmine*. However, among the religious buildings much greater interest undoubtedly surrounds the *Duomo* and the church of S. Francesco. The former, erected in the 11th century but entirely rebuilt in the 15th, has a distinctive three-storeyed bell-tower whose base lies on top of Roman architectural elements and culminates in a polychrome clock. In the interior, divided into a nave and two side aisles and enriched with elegant marble decoration, there is an impressive bishop's throne dating from 1573, a wooden choir masterfully inlaid by Sorrentino artisans, and numerous pictorial works. As for the 18th-century *church of S. Francesco*, this is particularly interesting for the elegant *cloister* of the adjoining conventual complex. Sober and harmonious, on two

sides 14th-century and clearly inspired by a design of Arabic origin, and on the other two lined with octagonal pilasters supporting round arches, it offers a delightful view of the bell-tower, which culminates in a distinctive cusp. But in actual fact the entire historic centre of Sorrento has a wealth of fascinating features: the narrow streets, paved in stone, the typical palaces studded with balconies, and the houses joined to each other by means of slender arches that betray their medieval origin. Here we find the characteristic 15th-century loggia, which the aristocracy used for a long time as the meeting-place for debating the city's most important affairs. The elegant maiolica cupola that crowns it and the refined 17th-century frescoes adorning its interior reconfirm, if ever there was any need, the public function held by what is curiously known as the *Sedile Dominova*.

Of considerable interest, finally, is the *Museo Correale di Terranova*, housed in the 18th-century palace of the same name, surrounded by a luxuriant park with a terrace looking out over an enchanting panorama. Displayed in the museum are what were once the collections of the brothers Alfredo and Pompeo Correale, counts of Terranova, consisting of paintings of the Neapolitan school, Greco-Roman finds, medieval works of art, as well as the best production of the lesser arts, Neapolitan and non, of the 16th, 17th and 18th centuries.

But Sorrento remains above all a seaside town, even though the high coastline has practically deprived it of any particularly large beaches and a proper sea-front. At *Marina Grande* and *Marina Piccola* one descends by way of underpasses and flights of steps to reach the tourist landing-places, the brightly-coloured

The old Duomo of Sorrento contains marble decorations and solemn furnishings which are flanked by the pictorial division of the ceiling of the nave and transept. Note also the highly characteristic three-storeyed bell-tower surmounted by a belfry that must originally have housed the bells.

The charm of Sorrento derives mainly from the sea, with the landing-stages of the splendid Marina Grande and the smaller Marina Piccola. Among the peculiarities of this town, in addition to its thriving and extremely varied handicrafts industry, we should also mention the Sedile Dominova, a refined 15th century loggia culminating in a maiolica-decorated cupola whose interior is embellished with elegant decorations.

bathing establishments with cabins and sunshades arranged on piles and on the breakwater rocks, and the little fishing harbour, animated by a fervent and uninterrupted activity. Marina Piccola, particularly, is the most important wharf of the city: motorships and hydroplanes draw alongside here, pleasure craft enthusiasts moor here, and from here the tourist arriving by sea from Naples discovers the unique charm of a seaside city suspended on a terrace of tufa.

Not far from Sorrento, in the area of Punta del Capo, are the remains of a Roman building that still preserves traces of structures used for bathing. This is, in all probability, the **Villa of Pollius Felix**, which was frequently described by the Roman poet Statius. It stood near the sea, not far from that crack in the rock which has let the seawater trickle in to form the picturesque basin known as **Queen Joan's Bath**.

MASSA LUBRENSE, MARINA DELLA LOBRA, S. AGATA SUI DUE GOLFI

The extreme tip of the Sorrento Peninsula opens out into a green basin containing the pleasant holiday resort of **Massa Lubrense**. Of ancient Longobard origin, the town is dominated by the *church of S. Maria delle Grazie*, which was built in 1512, restructured in the 18th century, and is embellished with a splendid maiolica pavement (18th century). The name of the town comes from the word "mass", with which the groups of lands and rural dwellings were indicated in the Middle Ages, and from the Latin word "delubrum", which refers to the presence of an ancient temple, possibly consecrated to Minerva. Destroyed first by Charles of Anjou (1336) and later by the king of Naples Ferdinando I (1464), it was subsequently invaded by the Turks (1558). Awarded the title of principal-

The suggestive sanctuary of S. Maria della Lobra, with a detail of the lavishly decorated ceiling; and, of different though no lesser charm, of Queen Joan's Bath, near to which one can admire the remains of the Villa of Pollius Felix.

Massa Lubrense dominates the sea from the top of its verdant rounded hillside. The most tourist-frequented, though no less interesting part of the town is the seaside village of Marina della Lobra, which has a small harbour and little beach and is dominated by the 16th-century profile of the sanctuary of S. Maria della Lobra.

ity in 1645, two years later it played an active role in the popular uprising of Masaniello. Today it is above all a busy fishing port and a well-frequented seaside resort, favoured by a splendid coast where we find **Marina della Lobra**, a small fishing village equipped with tourist landing-stages. The town is dominated by the 16th-century *sanctuary of S. Maria della Lobra*, where a wooden Crucifix of the 18th century is preserved.

Further inland, straddling a ridge from which the view ranges as much over the Gulf of Naples as it does over that of Salerno, stands a pleasant little village with the unequivocal name **S. Agata sui Due Golfi**. The place is interesting for the 17th-century *church of S. Maria delle Grazie*, which houses a magnificent high altar in polychrome marble. The work of Florentine artists of the 16th century, the altar is adorned with resplendent semi-precious stones and mother-of-pearl. Particularly well-known and much frequented, contrary to what the name would suggest, is the *Desert*, once a Carmelite hermitage, then an orphanage, but today the favourite place for appreciating what are still the principal attractions of S. Agata: the views.

ISOLE DE LI GALLI, MARINA DEL CANTONE, PONTE DEI LIBRI, GROTTA MATERA

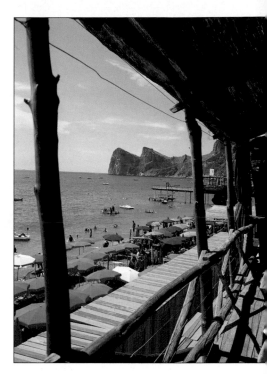

Rugged cliffs, enchanting inlets, villages suspended between the rocks and the sea: this is the delightful scenery of the **Amalfi Coast**, which juts out towards the Tyrrhenian Sea almost held up by the ridge of the Monti Lattari. Among its many virtues, besides the undoubted beauty of the landscape and an extraordinarily mild climate, a glorious centuries-old history. For a long time, under the protection of the unrivalled power of the Maritime Republic of Amalfi, this entire rocky area, lined with terraces cultivated with olives, vineyards and citrus orchards, enjoyed great splendour and an enviable prosperity. The rock, the main feature of the coast, is particularly friable. This, therefore, has given rise to the creation of veritable fjords, carved by the streams in their course towards the sea, and of many beaches, formed from the rocky material that detaches from the cliffs and crumbles into pebbly detritus.

From Punta Campanella the view is lost over the limpid sea, from which the characteristic rocks emerge known as the **Isole de Li Galli** or **Isole Sirenuse** since this, according to legend, was the actual dwelling-place of the mythical Sirens who dazzled Ulysses. Today the four rocks - Gallo Lungo, Castelluccia, Rotonda and Vetara - are popular attractions for boating trips, the favourite departure-point being from **Marina del Cantone**. Surrounded by vineyards and citrus orchards and dominated by the ancient *look-out post of Montalto*, this village boasts the largest beach of the entire Sorrento Peninsula.

The scenic itinerary of savage beauty continues towards Positano: snaking its way high above the sea and penetrating here and there into the rock, it

In a sea of crystalline azure, one of the incomparable beauties of the Amalfi Coast, are four unmistakable rocks called the Isole de Li Galli.

MAIOLICAS OF THE COAST

One of the most prized and celebrated products of the handicrafts of the Amalfi Coast are its vividly coloured maiolicas and tiles. Used for innumerable architectural decorations, they form an integral part of every panoramic view of the area.

The maiolica-decorated bench back of the celebrated Hotel S. Pietro, with Positano in the background.

The town of Positano rises vertically, with its typical cube-shaped houses climbing up the hillside terraces that slope down towards the sea. It is no surprise, therefore, that the town's streets are frequently replaced by flights of steps, that the houses seem almost to be stacked one on top of the other, and that the beaches often lie at the bottom of steep cliffs.

leads to the discovery of unique places, like **Ponte dei Libri**, flanked by high pinnacles and so called because of the various layers of rock that resemble the pages of a book; or the **Grotta Matera**, into which the sea penetrates deeply.

POSITANO

Positano looks as if it had actually climbed up the sloping terraces of Monte Comune and Monte S. Angelo ai Tre Pizzi. It is no coincidence that the famous painter Paul Klee, when describing the town, called it the "only place in the world conceived on a vertical rather than a horizontal axis".
Its characteristic cube-shaped houses - painted in white, pink, ochre and orange, and often preceded by a small portico, immersed in the greenery

84

and joined together more by flights of steps than by real roads - look down over a small beach.

Tradition has it that the name of Positano is derived from that of Paestum, whose inhabitants, fleeing from a Saracen attack, were said to have founded the town. What is certain is that it came to rival Amalfi in prosperity and importance in the sphere of maritime trade, and that in the 19th century it became one of the most exclusive holiday resorts. A vocation, this, that Positano has astutely succeeded in maintaining and revitalizing: favoured, in the first half of the 20th century, by artists and intellectuals - Gorki, Cocteau, Picasso and Lenin - today the town offers tourists first-class hotels, splendid beaches, including *Marina Grande*, a lively cultural climate boosted by interesting exhibitions such as the Musical Festival, flourishing handicrafts ranging

The enchanting Grotta dello Smeraldo and the Fjord of Furore, with its suggestive Nordic charm.

from lace-working to wine-making, and so on up to the characteristic brightly-coloured maiolicas whose luminous elegance enlivens many corners of the town. Coloured maiolica, in fact, embellishes the cupola of S. Maria Assunta, the parish church that dominates Positano, whose interior, divided by a nave and two side aisles, houses a 13th-century panel in the Byzantine style representing the "Madonna and Child". Also interesting is the medieval bas-relief of the bell-tower representing a sea monster, some fish and a fox.

Not very far from the inhabited centre is a grotto, **La Porta**, which is undoubtedly worth a visit. Partly caved in following land subsidence, originally it must have been much larger than at present and in prehistory was inhabited from Palaeolithic times (15,000 years ago). It has yielded many interesting objects, including flint utensils and hunting instruments.

THE "GRAN FURORE"

One of the most celebrated and unforgettable peculiarities of the Fjord of Furore is the "Gran Furore Divina Costiera", a typical local wine obtained from vineyards cultivated in the vicinity of the villages of Furore and S. Elia.

FURORE, PRAIANO, CONCA DEI MARINI, GROTTA DELLO SMERALDO

Proceeding towards Amalfi, the road goes round the Vallone di Positano, dominated by the *Natural Arch*, a crevice in the rock just below Monte S. Angelo which in the morning, when the rays of the sun shine into it, gleams with a highly distinctive colour. Further on we come to an impressive series of small fjords, the result of a particular geological land formation and the centuries-old erosion of rivers. This is the case with the **Fjord of Furore**, which has been carved over the centuries by a torrent descending from the plateau of Agerola and today is crossed by a very high viaduct. Steep paths enable visitors to penetrate this wild valley and reach the village of **Furore**, closed in between steep flights of steps that lead to a solitary beach.

Beyond Vettica, a small seaside resort situated in a delightful position, between the steep rocky slope and the whiteness of the sandy shore, less solitary but equally suggestive is the not distant beach of **Praiano**, now a small village, but at the time of the Maritime Republic a centre of considerable splendour: the doges of the Republic spent their holidays in this locality and Charles I of Anjou wanted to estab-

The splendid beaches lining the coast between Conca dei Marini and Vettica di Praiano, with the elegant parish church rising against the background of the open sea, are an attractive foretaste of the enchanting beauty of Amalfi, a delightful view of which can be admired on the following page.

lish the University here, while the economy prospered thanks to flourishing manufacturing activities that produced highly-prized silks. Praiano declined with the fall in the fortunes of Amalfi, but succeeded in drawing on vital new resources from the systematic practice of fishing and the transformation of fish products, an activity which together with tourism still represents the mainstay of the town's economy. Today, evidence of its past glories can be seen in the *parish church of S. Luca*, which houses impressive 16th-century paintings attributed to Giovanni Bernardo Lama, together with the silver bust of S. Luca containing the venerated relics of the town's patron saint; and a *look-out post* erected in the Middle Ages to enable easier sightings of pirate ships.

Another tower, dating from the 16th century, stands at *Capo di Conca*, a rocky promontory that juts out between Praiano and Amalfi almost as if to defend the bay of **Conca dei Marini**, today a charming seaside resort but once a maritime port of prime importance endowed with a powerful mercantile fleet and the main naval base of nearby Amalfi.

Among the attractions of the place, besides the rustic little houses with their unmistakable barrel and cross vaults, is the fascinating **Grotta dello Smeraldo**, which gets its name from the distinctive colour of the water under the influence of the sun's refracted rays. The grotto, a large cavern measuring 60 metres by 30, which today can be visited in small boats, was discovered in 1932. Formerly dry in ancient times, it gradually became submerged by sea water following bradyseismic phenomena. The cave contains some extremely impressive stalagmites, which reach heights of up to ten metres, and an enchanting ceramic crib arranged on the bed of the grotto.

The town of Amalfi clinging to its rocky hillside, its small houses hemmed in between steep alleys and picturesque little squares. The patron saint of the town is S. Andrea, to whom the fountain of Piazza del Duomo is dedicated, of which a detail can be admired below.

AMALFI

In the distance, almost contested between the turquoise of the sea and the dark green of the rocky slopes, lies the splendid town of **Amalfi**, a picturesque tangle of small houses clinging to the characteristically steep and rocky little streets. Founded in the 6th century to offer shelter to groups of refugees fleeing from the Ostrogoths, Amalfi grew rapidly, favoured first by the protection and later by the disinterest of Byzantium, which earned it an unexpected independence. Later, after successfully resisting the attacks of the Longobards and Saracens, the city - which was established as an independent republic around 850 and ruled by magistrates holding the title of 'dukes', or 'doges' - became a leading commercial centre, backed by a well-equipped and powerful fleet. And while its jurisdiction extended to embrace the entire territory between Sorrento, Salerno and the Monti Lattari, its dominion over the central and eastern Mediterranean continued unaltered until the end of the 11th century. The conquest by the Normans and the two sacks to which it was subjected in 1135 and 1137 by its old-time rival, Pisa, marked the end of its republi-

The Duomo of Amalfi dominates the town's piazza from the top of a flight of 62 steps. The building is graced by a splendid airy atrium of Gothic inspiration, and an elegant high altar surmounted by a statue of S. Andrea.

can freedoms and the beginning of an inexorable decline. Over the centuries the old town was heavily damaged by devastating sea-storms (the one of 1343 being particularly bad), the harbour got smaller, the victim of continual erosion, and the beach also suffered the same fate. Today, dotted with interesting monuments that seem to stand as evidence of ancient glories, Amalfi is above all a pearl of art and a famous holiday resort, in which the gaily-coloured houses blend with the vivid hues of the enchanting natural surroundings. There are impressive remains of the *Arsenal of the Republic*, today divided into two large halls, where the majestic, and for the time extremely modern galleys of the fleet were built. Also noteworthy, though for different reasons, is the ceramic panel near the *Porta della Marina* representing an old nautical chart of the south-eastern Mediterranean; and the hotels - especially Hotel Luna - obtained from old Franciscan and Capuchin convents, whose austere cloisters have survived and can be visited. But the real artistic jewel of the town is certainly the splendid *Duomo*, which stands on the piazza named after it, the true heart of the city, revolving around the 18th-century Baroque fountain

called the Fontana del Popolo or Fontana di S. Andrea. To the same saint - who, according to legend, saved Amalfi from the Saracens by rousing up a terrible sea-storm in 1544 - the cathedral is also dedicated, built in the 9th century but several times modified and even rebuilt in both the 13th and 18th centuries. The bell-tower, pierced by a tracery of two-light and three-light windows, was erected between 1180 and 1270, while the fa cade, heavily damaged in 1861, was rebuilt in the original style and decorated with a mosaic representing "Christ Enthroned". Particularly accentuated Arabo-Norman forms are thus interwoven with the Gothic style of the atrium and the Baroque magnificence of the interiors. Note the distinctive central *portal* in bronze embossed with silver, cast in Constantinople in 1066, the fascinating *Chapel of the Crucifix*, undoubtedly the best-conserved part of the entire edifice with its capitals decorated with historical scenes, and the crypt, decorated with the statues of Pietro Bernini. Particularly fine - as its name suggests - is the *Cloister of Paradise*, with its luxuriant central garden. Here the charm and elegance of the clear Arabic influence coexist with sarcophagi and sculptures of the Roman and medieval period and with the large fresco of the "Crucifixion" executed in 1330, almost 70 years after the construction of the same cloister, by a Neapolitan painter, Roberto d'Oderisio.

ATRANI, RAVELLO, SCALA, MAIORI, MINORI

Historically linked to the fortunes of nearby Amalfi, **Atrani** opens like an amphitheatre overlooking the sea, with the *cathedral of S. Maria Maddalena* dominated by a maiolica cupola and by the bizarre bell-tower culminating in a two-storeyed octagonal belfry. But the religious building of greatest interest is the *church of S. Salvatore*, which for a long time housed the official cerimonies of investiture and burial of the doges of the Republic. Note the particularly impressive portal which was cast in Constantinople in 1087.

The power of Amalfi was also decisive for the fortunes of **Ravello**, an elegant town lying on the flat summit of a hill, which in its period of greatest splendour had a population of 30,000 inhabitants, compared to the 2,600 of today. But sackings and pestilence, which were capable of annihilating its power, could do nothing against the most prestigious symbols of an extremely animated history and culture: the *Duomo of S. Pantaleone* (11th century), a sober, elegant building with a stupendous bronze portal dating from 1179; in the three-naved interior, precious works of art, like the majestic marble pulpit (1272) decorated with mosaics, friezes and columns, the silver statue of S. Pantaleone, the patron saint of the city, chased in 1759 and preserved in the homonymous chapel, and the flask containing the saint's blood, which liquefies every year on 27 July, the anniversary of his martyrdom; the imposing *Villa Rufolo*, with its unmis-

The town of Atrani, charmingly arranged like an amphitheatre on the seashore, is dominated by the cathedral of S. Maria Maddalena with its slender and vividly-coloured maiolica cupola.

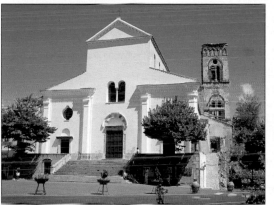

Ravello is distinguished by the sober elegance of the Duomo of S. Pantaleone, with its stupendous bronze portal composed of 54 panels, and by the imposing Villa Rufolo, with its intriguing Arabo-Norman style.

WAGNER AT RAVELLO

The enchanting atmosphere of the garden terrace of Villa Rufolo, at Ravello, provided the celebrated German composer Richard Wagner with the inspiration for the pages of "Parsifal" on the magic garden of Klingsor. In commemoration of this noble fact, the place was chosen to host the annual summertime Wagnerian concerts and musical performances that have become internationally renowned.

The gardens of Villa Rufolo.

takable Arabo-Norman style, built in the 13th century by the wealthy family of Roman origin whose name it carries to this day and embellished by a splendid garden full of exotic plants; and lastly, the bizarre *Villa Cimbrone*, a 20th-century construction in the medieval style enjoying an enviable panoramic position.

As for the numerous small villages lining this stretch of coast, the course of their history is once again constantly influenced by the alternating fortunes of Amalfi. This is true of **Scala**, a group of small villages of Roman origin which, despite repeated sackings, experienced a considerable expansion during the centuries of the Maritime Republic. The *cathedral of S. Lorenzo*, whose present Baroque style is due to successive alterations, dates from this period. It is also the case with **Maiori** and **Minori**, the ancient Reginna Maior and Reginna Minor, lying in a natural amphitheatre of hills overlooking a splendid bay. The *church of S. Maria a Mare*

95

The mock medieval style of Villa Cimbrone, at Ravello, looks rather unusual given that the building was constructed in the present century. Minori is noteworthy for its characteristic urban architecture, while Maiori is distinguished by the powerful structure of its old Norman tower.

at Maiori, with its great maiolica cupola, and the remains of an ancient Roman villa at Minori, dating from the 1st century BC - comprising the courtyard, the swimming pool with a hydraulic installation, the flight of steps, the terraces and some rooms, which today contain interesting remains of other constructions - are some of the main attractions of what are two of the most popular seaside resorts in the area.

VIETRI SUL MARE AND CAVA DEI TIRRENI

Proceeding eastwards along a harsh and rugged coast, we cross Capo d'Orso and come to a locality of extremely ancient origin, **Vietri sul Mare**, the Etruscan Marcina, which suffered the domination of the Samnites, the Lucanians and the Romans, the destruction of the Vandals and the favour of the Longobards, as well as the inevitable Saracen sackings. Situated in one of the most beautiful and suggestive areas of the

Vietri sul Mare, a charming seaside resort, has always cultivated a flourishing ceramic craft industry. The history and name of the nearby Cava dei Tirreni is linked to the centuries-old abbey of S. Trinità della Cava.

coast, immersed in the greenery of a lush vegetation, Vietri today is a picturesque seaside resort boasting some impressive monuments - the *church of S. Giovanni Battista* and the *Arciconfraternita dell'Annunziata e del Rosario* - and with a thriving traditional handicraft production of ceramics which traces its origins to the Middle Ages and to which the inhabitants of the town have dedicated a museum, housed at Raito, in the tower of *Villa Guariglia*.

A few kilometres inland, a geographical depression with an extremely mild climate and extraordinarily fertile soil is occupied by the busy town of **Cava dei Tirreni**, an agricultural centre of prime importance for the production of cereals, fruit, tobacco and prized wines, but also the centre of textile, furniture and tobacco manufactures. Not far away stands the *Benedictine abbey of S. Trinità della Cava*, founded in 1011 by the friar Alferio from Cluny, who chose a cave as the early site, hence the name 'Cava' which was extended to the whole inhabited area. The town remained under the abbey's jurisdiction for centuries before obtaining the title of city and the relative autonomy from Pope Boniface IX.

SALERNO

Further east along the homonymous gulf is **Salerno**, the provincial centre which in antiquity was the seat of a celebrated School of Medicine, the first to be set up in Europe with declared didactic ends and certainly one of the most long-lasting, if, after being founded in the 9th century, it was suppressed only in 1811 by Joachim Murat. Developing from the Roman colony of Salernum, the city still has its characteristic medieval centre culminating in the grandiose Norman *Duomo*, which Robert Guiscard had built in 1076-1085 and decorated with marbles and sculptures from Paestum. The building, which has been modified various times, boasts numerous precious attractions: the artistic porticoed atrium, the Romanesque bell-tower of the mid-12th century, the portal adorned with marble friezes known as the *Porta dei Leoni*, the Byzantine-style mosaics, the ambos with mosaic decoration and the *tomb of Margherita d'Anjou Durazzo*. No less interesting are the *churches of S. Giorgio* and *S. Maria delle Grazie*, the former Baroque, the latter 15th century, which contain precious examples of sacred art. Around such an illustrious past, in recent times Salerno has developed a flourishing economy supported by the vital contribution of the large harbour and by the undeniable potential of tourism.

Standing in the modern urban fabric of the busy city of Salerno is the distinctive and austere mass of the old Norman Duomo, with its elaborate architecture and precious works of art.

PAESTUM

At the southern end of the Piana del Sele, not far from the mouth of the Sele river, the presence of numerous prehistoric finds has confirmed the presence of human settlements here from as long ago as the Neolithic Period. In the 7th century BC, in the same place, on a low travertine terrace, Greek colonists from Sibari founded Poseidonia, a settlement which immediately experienced rapid demographic, urbanistic and economic expansion, the latter in particular linked to a flourishing trade in cereals and oil. Falling under the dominion of the Lucanians in 400 BC, probably as a result of fairly violent actions of conquest, as is suggested by the traces of fire still recognizable in some temples, in 273 BC Poseidonia surrendered to the power of Rome and thus saw the new name, Paistom, which the Lucanians had given it, Latinized into **Paestum**.

The Romans gave the city a long period of splendid prosperity, integrating into the characteristically Greek monumental urban structure those civil and religious structures that were typical of every Roman colony: the Agora was flanked by the Forum, the Greek gods by those of the Romans. The fortunes of Paestum remained substantially unaltered until the threshold of the Middle Ages, when a slow and inexorable decline set in. Forced to flee initially from the gradual spread of malaria and later by the intensification of Saracen raids, the population finished by abandoning the ancient settlement to centuries of oblivion. In fact, with the exception of the plundering carried out in the 11th century by Robert Guiscard, who used its marbles and sculptures to embellish the Duomo of Salerno, Paestum remained practically forgotten about at least until the 18th century, when the first excavations were undertaken and the monuments were rebaptized with the names that distinguish them today. At the present time, over 200 years later, only the central area of the ancient city has been completely brought to light, including numerous *insulae* of the Hellenistic-Roman age reserved for private dwellings. Many areas, now belonging to private owners, have not yet been explored: it is possible to form an idea of their size thanks to the perfect preservation of the city's perime-

An aerial view showing the size and magnificence of the archeological area of Paestum, dotted with ancient and imposing monuments.

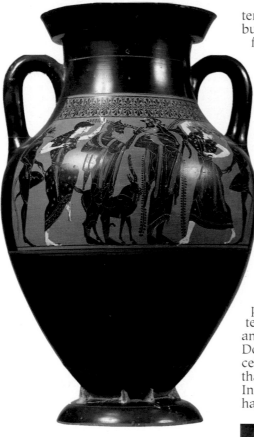

ter wall, within whose boundary they were and are situated. These *walls*, built in the 4th centruy BC and later several times restructured and reinforced, run for a length of 5 km, flanked by a defensive ditch, forming a sort of pentagon. In them there are 4 main gates, 47 secondary openings and 28 defensive towers, today largely destroyed; the two that were subjected to substantial restoration in the course of the 19th century are easily identifiable.

Many of the grandiose buildings of Paestum trace their origins to an archaic period. This is true of the imposing *Basilica*, in actual fact a temple raised in honour of Hera around 550 BC, whose antiquity is confirmed by the numerous columns in travertine - 18 on the long sides and 9 along the fronts, made of superimposed rocks with a characteristic swelling in the middle - culminating in particularly squashed capitals made of limestone, like the architrave above. The large number of columns on the short sides, together with the total absence of pediments, suggested that the temple was a building used for secular affairs, thus earning it the name with which today it is conventionally known. The so-called *Temple of Neptune*, which due to its grandeur was mistakenly believed to be dedicated to the god that had given its name to the city - Poseidon (Neptune for the Roman world) - was also probably consecrated to Hera, or, according to other scholars, to Zeus. Built in around 450 BC, and surviving in a perfect state of conservation, the building is a perfect model of the Doric temple of the classical age: 14 columns on the long sides, 6 on the fronts, an architrave embellished with a decorated fascia and accompanied by a Doric frieze, triangular pediments on the short sides and, in the interior, a cella preceded by a pronaos composed of two columns between antae that support a frieze.

In antiquity the sacred area was enclosed by a wall whose foundations have survived. To the west of the area of the temples, this wall marked

The Temple of Neptune, the best preserved of the entire archeological area, stands next to the Basilica. On the opposite page, below, the Temple of Ceres. Among the numerous finds that have been brought to light at Paestum are the black-figure Attic amphora found in the Heroon of the Agora (above), and the funerary paintings, an example of which is shown below.

the beginning of the *Via Sacra*, a wide paved street traversed by processions, to the left of which long blocks of residential quarters dating from the Roman period have been brought to light. The street also ran alongside the vast flat area of the *Forum*, whose original structure dates from the 3rd century BC. Overlooking the Forum were long rows of *tabernae*, the characteristic rectangular shops sometimes provided with an upper floor. Interrupting this picturesque line on the south side was the *Curia*, the place set aside for the administration of justice, and the *Macellum*, which had the function of an open market; on the north side the *Comitium*, built around 273 BC to house the assembly of citizens, and the *Italic Temple*, also known as the *Temple of Peace*, but probably dedicated to the Capitoline Triad of Jupiter, Juno and Minerva, built in the 2nd century BC. Behind the monuments of the Forum, eastwards, stood the great *Amphitheatre*, built in the 1st century BC, of which only the western half is visible today. Immediately to the north of the Amphitheatre, a portico still marks the southern boundary of what was the *Agora*, the true heart of the Greek city. Replaced by the Forum in the Roman period and stripped of all its functions, the square was practically abandoned, only to be later

The aerial views enable us to appreciate fully the monumentality of the temples of Paestum. The metopes of the frieze from the Great Temple of the Heraion of Foce Sele is evidence of the refinement achieved by local artists.

set aside, in the imperial age, as the area for residential quarters. Two of its main monuments are still visible: the *Hypogean Sacellum* - datable to 510 BC, embedded in a bank of rock, covered by a double sloping roof and totally devoid of any openings - which must have formed a heroon-cenotaph, the symbolic tomb of the founder of Poseidonia, becoming the object of a heroic cult; and the *Bouleuterion*, built around 470 BC, used for housing the public assemblies of citizens.

Proceeding along the Via Sacra in a northerly direction we reach the northern sanctuary of the city, named thus in order to distinguish it from the area of temples to the south, and dominated by the so-called *Temple of Ceres*, which in actual fact was consecrated to Athena, as is confirmed by the numerous statuettes representing the armed goddess discovered in the votive deposits around the building. Built in around 500 BC, it represents an element of transition between the late-Archaic temples and those of the classical age. Only the foundations of the cella remain today, while the medieval tombs that have been brought to light around it make it highly likely that the entire building was transformed into a Christian church at the dawn of the Middle Ages.

In the middle of the ancient city, the interesting new *National Archeological Museum* was set up in 1952, housing a very rich collection of finds that have come to light in the course of excavations. These range from vases, ceramics, statues, fragments of buildings and decorations from the temples (among these the so-called *Heraion of Foce Sele*, the sanctuary of Hera that lay 10 km north of Poseidonia on the left bank of the river Sele, proving the absolute pre-eminence attributed to the cult of this god in the area), to large painted tombs. Celebrated among these the so-called *Tomb of the Diver*, for which the museum has reserved a special room. The only evidence of funerary art in Poseidonia in the 5th century BC, this simple coffin tomb, closed by a flat covering, betrays a clear Etruscan influence in the practice of decorating the internal walls with fresco paintings. Among the convivial scenes represented, on the covering slab is the figure of a naked man diving into water: an evocative symbolic representation of the passage from life to death that has given its name to the entire burialplace.

Some of the precious finds preserved in the Archeological Museum of Paestum, including the magnificent fresco paintings of the celebrated Tomb of the Diver, true masterpieces of elegant simplicity.

AGROPOLI, CASAL VELINO, VELIA, PISCIOTTA, PALINURO, MARINA DI CAMEROTA, SCARIO, SAPRI

On a promontory just south of Paestum - from which the panorama ranges towards the Gulf of Salerno and on whose beaches tradition has it that St Paul landed in the course of his voyage towards Rome - lies **Agropoli**, an ancient centre founded by the Byzantines, dominated by the so-called *Saracen Castle*, whose name recalls the long period of Arab rule which lasted here from 882 to 1028. It seems to be no coincidence, therefore, the characteristic shape of the town's houses, which seem to avoid opening towards the outside, an ancient legacy of fears associated with dangers from the sea, in particular the continual raids of Saracen pirates. At the foot of the castle is the place which in antiquity must have been occupied by the *Greek sanctuary of Poseidon*, as numerous recent finds seem to confirm.

A view of the town and harbour of Agropoli, an ancient city situated on a high promontory.

EXPLORING THE CILENTO

Paestum is an open door to the Cilento hinterland, an area with well-defined morphological and climatic characteristics, so distinctive in fact that the National Park of the Cilento-Vallo di Diano has been instituted to safeguard its peculiarities. This is the most impervious part of Campania, but also one of the most attractive, where small villages perched on high ground stand out in the midst of vast shady expanses of olive groves. The alluvial plain known as the Vallo di Diano is particularly beautiful. Originally the basin of an old prehistoric lake and today traversed by the river Tanagro, the Vallo is an

Images of the Cilento: flora and fauna of the National Park, in which the characteristic village of Sacco is also located.

Below, the Great Cloister and elliptical stairway of the Certosa di S. Lorenzo at Padula, a village also notable for its monument to Giuseppe (Joe) Petrosino. Lastly, the 16th-century altarpiece from the church of the Annunziata at Teggiano.

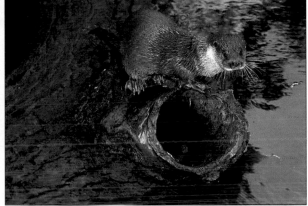

extremely fertile agricultural area with enchanting villages. Among these, Teggiano, which until 1862 was called Diano (hence the name of the entire zone), boasts a fine medieval castle and interesting religious buildings, like the 13th-century cathedral of S. Maria Maggiore. The picturesque Padula, situated on high ground at 700 m, is instead celebrated for the imposing Certosa di S. Lorenzo, built in 1306, several times enlarged over the centuries and finally completed only at the beginning of the 19th

century. Giuseppe Petrosino, who was born here in 1849, earned a place in legend for his activity in New York as the head of the Italian section of the international police, a fact today of which his home town seems particularly proud.

Proceeding further south, beyond **Casal Velino**, which is noteworthy for the attractive **Marina**, in the alluvial plain of the river Alento we come across the monumental ruins of ancient **Velia**, founded in the 6th century BC by the Phocaeans of Asia Minor, as testified by Herodotus and Strabo. Establishing itself as one of the most flourishing centres of Magna Graecia - the city was famous for its philosophers, particularly Parmenides and Zeno, who founded a famous and well-frequented school - in the Roman period, favoured by a very mild climate, it became a popular holiday resort, much liked by Cicero. The town's decline began to manifest in concomitance with the progressive sanding up of its two ports, to the point that in the Middle Ages the whole population had retired to the hill where in the 13th century the imposing Angevin tower was built. Even today the ancient *acropolis* is still easily identifiable on the rise, where the remains of houses dating from the 5th century BC are flanked by the ruins of a large *temple*, other smaller religious buildings and a little *theatre*. The perimeter walls of the city still run alongside this area, at the base of which are two distinct *quarters* joined by a road. The southern one, which in antiquity bordered the harbour, is notable for the presence - near a large semi-circular well that was possibly part of a

The mighty Angevin tower still keeps watch over the town of Velia. The imposing ruins of the old city overlooking the sea, and the splendid mosaics of the archeological area of Ascea.

108

The austere and suggestive town of Pisciotta, with its wide and very popular beach, a prelude to the enchanting scenery of Capo Palinuro with its high rocky coastline.

sanctuary dedicated to Eros - of a large *thermal building* dating from the 2nd century BC and of numerous interconnecting structures of the imperial age.

To reach the northern quarter one must go beyond the monumental *Porta Rosa*, which, since it was built in the second half of the 4th century BC, represents the oldest example of an ashlar arch in the whole of Magna Graecia.

Beyond Velia, again along the coastline, **Pisciotta**, situated among olive groves, is a prelude to the discovery of the small village of **Palinuro**,

More splendid images of Capo Palinuro, where an uncontaminated crystalline sea harmonizes with the charm of a wild and unspoilt landscape.

A PROMONTORY, A STORY

In the "Aeneid" Virgil narrates that Palinuro, the helmsman of the ship of Aeneas, caused to doze off by Juno, fell into the sea and three days later succeeded in reaching the Lucanian coast, where he was killed by the inhabitants of the place. To soothe his disconsolate shadow, which Aeneas meets in the Underworld, the Sibyl predicts an honoured burial by the hand of his own assassins, who are scourged by a plague, and the eternity of his memory, conserved in the name of the promontory that would house his tomb.

which almost clings to the homonymous cape that was made famous by Virgil's "Aeneid". Today its high rocky coasts, dotted with splendid grottos - which can only be visited by boat now but once, when the level of the sea was lower, were even used for living in - are an inevitable attraction for tourists.

Past this promontory, in a stupendous setting of orchards and olive groves, the seaside resorts of **Marina di Camerota, Scario** and **Sapri** mark the entrance to the north-western part of the Gulf of Policastro and the extreme southern limit of the Campanian coast. Marina di Camerota is a busy fishing centre also famous for the manufacture of amphoras, Scario is an outlying seaside hamlet of S. Giovanni a Piro, and Sapri is a charming town lying in a small bay whose economy is based on tourism, flourishing handicrafts and prosperous agricultural activity.

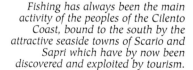

Fishing has always been the main activity of the peoples of the Cilento Coast, bound to the south by the attractive seaside towns of Scario and Sapri which have by now been discovered and exploited by tourism.

CASERTA AND ITS ROYAL PALACE

Charles of Bourbon, king of Naples and Sicily from 1734 to 1759 with the name of Charles VII, and then king of Spain with the name of Charles III, cherished an ambitious dream: that of giving his Italic possessions a new capital, substituting Naples and rivalling Versailles. He considered that the best way of realizing this objective was to start with the palace, whose execution was entrusted to the unquestionable talents of the celebrated papal architect Luigi Vanvitelli. Around the royal residence, 7 km away from the old city, the new city of **Caserta** would grow up in the second half of the 18th century, an unfinished example of a rationally conceived urban settlement, with broad rectilinear streets crossing each other at right-angles, laid out according to Vanvitelli's design. As for the palace, the first stone was officially laid by Charles of Bourbon himself on the day of his thirty-sixth birthday, 20 January 1752. At that time, the design stage had already been underway for a year and work was in progress on the definition of the spectacular surroundings of the future royal residence. For the occasion, the king made the imposing dimensions perceptible to all those present by lining up his troops along the perimeter of the palace under construction.

The project was begun enthusiastically, with the employment of 3000 men, and at the same time work was started on the construction of the monumental *Caroline Aqueduct* that was indispensable for the water supply of the enormous complex and its vast park. The design provided for an oblong building measuring 240 x 190 m, whose internal area was divided into four identical rectangular courts. Work proceeded rapidly until 1759, the year in which Charles VII of Bourbon was called to succeed his brother, who had died prematurely, on the Spanish throne. The throne of Naples was taken by Charles's third-born son, Ferdinando IV, an eight year-old child who was promptly entrusted to the tutelage of the prime minister Bernardo Tanucci, who was ill-disposed towards Vanvitelli and, more generally, towards unnecessary expenses. The work of constructing the new palace slowed down immediately, and was even interrupted in 1764, when Naples and its kingdom suffered a devastating famine. Thanks to an eruption of Vesuvius, which convinced the young king of the precariousness of his stay at Portici, work at Caserta was resumed in 1767, again under the supervision of Luigi Vanvitelli, flanked this time by his son Carlo who would succeed his father on the latter's death in 1773. It was Carlo Vanvitelli who finished the two main *facades*, the more austere one to the south, facing the city, and the

The Fountain of Venus and Adonis against the scenic background of the watercourse of the Palace of Caserta.

more picturesque one facing north towards the park. The hall of the main entrance on the side of the piazza is in perfect line with that of the park, with the watercourse of the garden and with the avenue leading towards Naples. The two halls are linked, inside the palace, by a long gallery, interrupted by an octagonal *central hall*, from which a monumental *stairway* begins. This corresponds on the upper floor with another octagonal hall which leads to the splendid *Chapel*, inaugurated on Christmas Day 1784 and honoured, on the occasion of another Christmas, that of 1849, by the presence of Pope Pius IX, who celebrated mass in it. Gleaming with marble throughout, it is clearly inspired by the Chapel of Versailles. On the same floor are the *Royal Apartments*, preceded by a series of majestic antechambers: in the first, the *Antechamber of the Halberdiers*, tower the marble busts of the queens; in the second, the *Antechamber of the Bodyguards*, those of the kings. The rooms of the 18th-century apartments follow, which start with the four dedicated to the seasons, embellished with fine pictorial decorations executed by Antonio Dominici and Fedele Fischetti. The *Studiolo of Ferdinando IV*, decorated 'all'antica' by Gaetano and Giuseppe Magri and Carlo Brunelli, leads to the *Salottino*, where the king assembled the Council, and then to the sovereigns' *Bedroom*. From here begins the *Queen's Apartment*, consisting of various rooms including the pretty *Room of the Stuccoes*, used for the queen's "toilette", a splendid bathroom and the *Boudoir of Maria Carolina*, used as the queen's reception.

On the eastern side of the palace were the rooms reserved for the young princes, adjacent to the lavish *Library*, organized into three rooms and stocked with some 14,000 books. It was the same queen Maria Carolina of Habsburg, the wife of Ferdi-

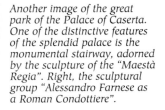

Another image of the great park of the Palace of Caserta. One of the distinctive features of the splendid palace is the monumental stairway, adorned by the sculpture of the "Maestà Regia". Right, the sculptural group "Alessandro Farnese as a Roman Condottiere".

116

nando IV, who was personally involved in its arrangement, in 1782. The shelves of the *First Room* are true masterpieces of cabinet-making, while the *Second Room* houses

two splendid *planispheres*, one celestial, the other terrestrial, executed in 1764 and in 1773 respectively by the French geographer Robert de Vaugondy.

In the west wing is the so-called *New Apartment*, completed in the 19th century. Two antechambers, the *Antechamber of Mars* and the *Antechamber of Astraea*, decorated between 1812 and 1815, lead to the *Throne Room*, 33 m long, 13 m wide and 16 m high. Finished in 1845 under the

Images of the Royal Palace: the sculpture representing the goddess of Justice in the Room of Astraea; the Library; the Throne Room; and the lavish gilded wooden throne.

supervision of Gaetano Genovese, it is superbly decorated with representations containing clear symbolic meanings. After the *Council Room* we come to the *Apartment of Francesco II*, which comprises, among its rooms, the *Wedding Chamber of Francesco II and Maria Sofia*, on whose ceiling Giuseppe Cammarano painted "The Rest of Theseus after his Fight with the Minotaur".

A strange object can be admired in the so-called backrooms of the 19th-century quarters: this is the celebrated *"flying chair"*, a seat of elevator raised by a hand-powered winch reserved for the exclusive use of Ferdinando

The crib which today is permanently set up in the Oval Room and an overall view of the sumptuous Palatine Chapel. In the park is the beautifully elaborate Fountain of Diana and Actaeon and the Fountain of Venus, of which an expressive detail is shown below.

IV, who with the Restoration became Ferdinando I of the Two Sicilies.

On the ground floor of the palace is the superb *Court Theatre*, literally demanded by Charles VII who forced Vanvitelli to modify part of his original design in order to include it. In it Ferdinando IV wanted to officially celebrate his wedding with Maria Carolina, but this never happened because the room was completed only in 1769, one year after the marriage. On the occasion of its inauguration, which coincided with Carnival festivities, all the highest-ranking nobility of the reign were invited, and from then on performances and representations were regularly held in it. Performances of a quite different kind, though equally appreciated, were organized in the "*Gran*

KING CHARLES' CRIB

O f all the traditions cultivated by the Bourbon rulers, the annual arrangement of the crib, in the Oval Room adjacent to the Library, was undoubtedly one of the most influential. Already Philip V of Spain had had statues of shepherds sent from Naples. His son, therefore, who became king of the Parthenopean city with the name of Charles VII, did not miss the opportunity to participate personally in the preparation of the crib, assisted by leading local artists. After him, all the Bourbon rulers enthusiastically continued this tradition, while the young princesses fitted out and embroidered the elaborate clothes of the characters. Today the Oval Room houses a monumental crib, whose arrangement in 1988 drew inspiration from the four views with which the court painter Salvatore Fergola represented the crib made in the Palace of Caserta for the Christmas of 1844.

The Bridge of Hercules, from which water descends into the Upper Fish-pond. Left, the luxuriant English garden and the basin of the Conca di Venere.

Piazza" in front of the entrance to the palace facing the city: parties and military parades were held here, with a great participation of crowds. A highly celebrated event was the "Tournament" for the 1846 Carnival, in which king Ferdinand II himself took part.

THE PARK. The magnificent *garden* starting in front of the north facade extends over an area of some 300 acres. Designed once again by Luigi Vanvitelli, although executed by his son Carlo, the park follows an ascending route which culminates in the monumental *Fountain of Diana and Actaeon*, whose marble sculptures are the work of Pietro and Tommaso Solari, Paolo Persico, Angelo Brunelli and Andrea Violani. From it gushes forth an impetuous cascade, inaugurated in 1768 in the presence of the newly-wed sovereigns Ferdinando and Maria Carolina. But dotted around the park are numerous other magnificent fountains, all the work of Gaetano Salomone or executed under his supervision: from the *Fountain of the Dolphins* to the one known as the

THE DUPLICATES OF CASERTA

It has been noted that in the Palace of Caserta it is not unusual to finds objects that are similar or even identical to others at the Palace of Versailles. It has been suggested that they were brought to Italy by surviving members of the French royal family, who at Caserta found refuge during the period of the Revolution after the decapitation of the sovereigns. But it is much more probable that they were the result of the frequent exchanges of gifts between the queen of Naples, Maria Carolina, and the queen of France, Marie-Antoinette, who were sisters, born within only three years of each other from the marriage of Maria Theresa of Austria and Francis Stephen of Lorraine.

CASERTAVECCHIA, S. ANGELO IN FORMIS, S. MARIA CAPUA VETERE, CAPUA

Still situated a few kilometres from the palace is the original, legitimate holder of the name "Caserta", which probably derives from the expression "Casa hirta", indicating an agglomeration perched on high ground. This is the picturesque medieval village clinging to the foot of Monte Virgo, which after the revolutionary urbanistic changes that gave rise to the modern Caserta in the second half of the 18th century, resigned itself, so to speak, to the name of **Casertavecchia**.

After the Longobard destruction of the prosperous city of Galatia, of ancient Etruscan origin, in the second

Palace of Aeolus, from the *Fountain of Ceres* to the *Fountain of Venus and Adonis*. In addition, on the explicit wishes of the queen Maria Carolina - who may have been influenced, as well as by the dictates of fashion, also by the English plenipotentiary at the court of Naples, Lord Hamilton - in 1786 the botanist John Andrew Graefer arrived from London, charged with laying out an *English garden*, an enchanting oasis dedicated to the goddess of beauty, where the basin of the *Conca di Venere* is followed by the *Little Swan Lake*, and where greenhouses alternate with nurseries, which were immediately installed for the cultivation of exotic plants: here, among other things, grew the first camelia plant, brought from Japan by the monk Kamel.

The splendid austere cathedral of S. Michele Arcangelo at Casertavecchia, with its powerful octagonal lantern.

The church of S. Angelo, the ancient basilica of S. Angelo in Formis, notable for the decorations of the facade and for the frescoes adorning the interiors, particularly the vault of the apse.

half of the 9th century, its inhabitants found refuge on this hill and founded a new settlement. Later ruled by the Normans, Caserta expanded rapidly and in the 12th century became a fief of the Sanseverino family. It was in this period that its *castle*, which was often occupied by the emperor Frederick II, was supplemented with the mighty cylindrical tower standing on a polygonal base. The town was later ruled by the Pignatelli, Belmonte, Braherio, Caetani and Della Ratta families and finally by the Acquaviva family, who in the 17th century triggered the decline of the old Caserta, preferring the mighty Longobard tower, converted into a place, that stood in the plain near Torre, not far from where a century later the great royal palace would be built.

Today the village of Casertavecchia still preserves unaltered its austere medieval charm, with its *cathedral of S. Michele Arcangelo*, built in the 12th century using materials from the nearby Temple of the Tifatine Jupiter. In it the Romanesque structure clearly shows

traces of Siculo-Muslim influences, but also more typically Apulian and Lombard elements. The building has a distinctive octagonal lantern, while the cupola, a splendid expression of the more mature Siculo-Campanian style, was executed in the 13th century. To the right of the cathedral stands the rectangular bell-tower, completed in 1234. Inside the church are numerous splendid tombs, including that of bishop Giacomo Martono (14th century), that of count Francesco Della Ratta (14th century) and that of the Casertan nobleman Ortensio Giaquinto (16th century). Just behind the cathedral stands the 14th-century *church of the Annunziata*, originally provided with a small hospital.

Around Casertavecchia is a fertile plain where the rectlinear layout of the roads which cross at rightangles reveals the rational geometric division of agricultural land worked by the Romans. A regularity, this, that is also reflected, inevitably, in the structure of the urban centres of what was significantly known as the *Campania Felix*. This is true of **S. Angelo in Formis**, at the foot of Monte Tifata. An ancient residential appendix of nearby Capua, today the small town huddles around the homonymous *church*, an austere basilica built between 1072 and 1099 on the wishes of the abbot of Montecassino where the Temple of the Tifatine Diana stood in antiquity. Note the impressive cycle of frescoes that decorate its interior commissioned by abbot Desiderio, who is represented in the apse, where there is also an image of Christ enthroned surrounded by symbols of the evangelists.

Nearby, the ancient Oscan, and later Etruscan, settlement of Capua, which under the Romans developed into one of the most heavily-populated centres of the empire, today has the name of **S. Maria Capua Vetere** and the appearance of a modern town, characterized by wide streets and an extremely regular ground-

THE GAY LIFE OF CAPUA

Vestiges of Roman Capua.

Life in ancient Capua was so splendid and easy that even Hannibal's soldiers were unable to resist its seductive charms. While waiting to march on Rome, in the winter between 216 and 215 BC, the Carthaginian troops stayed in the town at length. Later, the vulnerability they demonstrated in the subsequent conflict with the Romans was attributed to the lascivious and dissolute life they conducted here. Today, more than 2000 years later, the "gay life of Capua" survives as a proverbial expression to indicate a state of dissipation preventing someone from reaching a specific objective.

The majestic remains of the Amphitheatre at S. Maria Capua Vetere.

THE VOLTURNO

The Volturno river appears to flow peacefully in the Campanian plain, describing numerous meanders and encircling Capua in a tight bend, but in the course of the centuries it has been the scene of several bloody battles. The first involved the Byzantine troops of Narsete, who in 554 defeated the Franco-Alemannian troops of Butilino here. Later it was the turn of Garibaldi's soldiers, who on the banks of the river between the 1st and 2nd of October 1860 victoriously opposed the Bourbon army led by general Ritucci. More recently, between the 13th and 14th of October 1943, the American 5th Army defeated the XIV German Panzerkorps along the final stretch of the river, thus opening the road towards Rome.

The Volturno river.

plan. Destroyed by the Saracens in the 9th century, it rose again around the surviving *basilica di S. Maria Maggiore*, a vast church with five naves several times modified in the 17th and 18th centuries, which until 1862 gave its name to the entire town. Note the imposing remains of the *Campanian Amphitheatre* (2nd century AD), comparable in size to the Colosseum in Rome, the interesting ancient *Baths*, the *Honorary Arch* on the Via Appia and the large *sanctuary* (4th century BC) which housed the celebrated "matres matutae", statues of women with children today conserved at the *Museo Campano* of modern **Capua**.

Capua is a flourishing town that was founded in the 9th century on the site of ancient Casilinum, 4 km away from Etruscan Capua, by the latter's inhabitants. The town is situated on the left bank of the Volturno and has a beautiful medieval *Duomo*; dedicated to SS. Stefano e Agata, several times modified and entirely rebuilt first in the 18th century and again after the devastating bombardments of the Second World War, it still conserves a delightful atrium supported by 20 columns dating from the 3rd century, and a 9th-century bell-tower adorned with a splendid tracery of marbles and two-light mullioned windows. But in the urban fabric of Capua there are numerous churches which are as much of Longobard and Norman origin (from *S. Salvatore Maggiore a Corte* to *S. Angelo Audoaldis*) as of clear Baroque design. Also noteworthy is the so-called *"Castello delle Pietre"*, an ancient palace of the Norman princes, the *Triumphal Arch of Frederick II*, the *Town Hall* and the *Palazzo Fieramosca*, which gets its name from the celebrated condottiere Ettore Fieramosca who died in Spain in 1515.

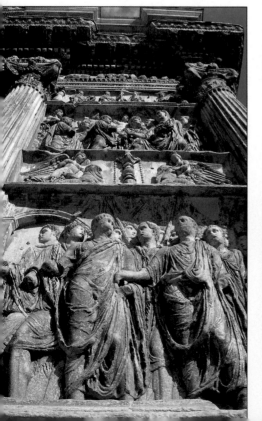

The majestic Triumphal Arch of Trajan, at Benevento, entirely decorated with imposing and elegant reliefs.

THE SANNIO

BENEVENTO, MONTESARCHIO, MIRABELLA ECLANO, MONTEVERGINE, PIETRELCINA

A vast region with a complex orohydrographical structure and with a mountainous terrain cloaked in woods, in antiquity the **Sannio** was the homeland of the powerful and bellicose Italic people known as the Samnites, who in the 5th century BC set out from here to conquer southern Italy. Administratively divided between Campania, Molise and Abruzzo, today it is an area of considerable touristic interest, favoured by its unquestionable natural beauty and by the presence of enchanting towns and villages. The Campanian part of the Sannio is distinguished by the presence of **Benevento**, a city with an illustrious historical past: for a long time it was a principality, first under the Longobards and the Franks, and much later under Napoleon, with a long interlude - almost eight centuries - of direct papal rule. Capital of the Irpinian Samnites with the

The bed of Padre Pio.

THE BIRTHPLACE OF PADRE PIO

Among the illustrious offspring of the Sannio region, one man has recently had his own heroic virtues recognized by the Vatican authorities, the ritual prelude to the elevation to sainthood, somehow anticipated by the diffusion of a heartfelt popular devotion. This is a Capuchin friar whose own life - marked by extraordinary events, like the appearance of the stigmata in 1918 - is linked to the convent of S. Giovanni Rotondo, near Foggia, where he lived from 1916 and where he died in 1968. But this fervent religious man always kept in his name a clear reference to his birthplace, being remembered in the history of the Church as Padre Pio of Pietrelcina.

Above, the monumental remains of the Amphitheatre at Benevento. Below, the village of Montesarchio, lying at the foot of the fortified medieval castle.

name of Maleventum, it was subsequently given the more auspicious name of Beneventum by the Romans, grateful for having defeated the troops of Pyrrhus here in 275 BC. For Benevento the period of Roman rule coincided with a phase of great prosperity: splendid evidence of this can be seen in the remains of the *Amphitheatre* and in the magnificent *Triumphal Arch of Trajan* (2nd century AD), which is almost 16 m high and decorated all over with elaborate bas-reliefs. Dating from the medieval age are the city *walls*, the *castle*, and above all the *cathedral* with its five naves, erected in the 7th century but entirely rebuilt first between the 9th and 13th centuries and again in 1959, after the devastating German bombardments of 1943. As for the austere 8th-century *church of S. Sofia in Voto*, with adjoining convent, one of the finest examples of medieval architecture in Europe, tradition has it that it was built on the site where the witches of the city were accustomed to meet. Benevento is also the seat of the interesting *Museum of the Sannio*, which houses precious archeological collections and medieval and modern art.

There are, however, numerous localities of great interest in the Sannio. **Montesarchio**, for example, at the foot of Monte Taburno, already fortified in the Roman period and a site of considerable strategic importance in the period of the barbarian invasions, ruled by the Normans and the Swabians and later the fief of the D'Aquino and Carafa families, it is still dominated by the imposing mass of the medieval *castle* which from a dominant position keeps an austere vigil over the Valle Caudina. Not far away, **Mirabella Eclano** embodies in its name a reference to the ancient Roman colony that was established exactly 15 miles from Benevento and destroyed by Saracens and Normans - Eclano - as well as a reference to the district that was the fief of the Visconti and Sforza families. Situated on the right bank of the river Calore, the town is noteworthy today for the impressive *Mother Church*, which houses a wooden Crucifix of the 12th century; and for the *church of the Annunziata*, in whose interior artistic papier-mâché reproductions of scenes from the Passion can be admired.

A place of great popular devotion is the sanctuary of **Montevergine**, an old Benedictine monastic centre built by S. Guglielmo da Vercelli in 1119 under the summit of the limestone massif known also as the Partenio. In the new *basilica*, opened to the cult in 1961, the Madonna of Montevergine is venerated, a 13th-century painting of Byzantine inspiration.

Another centre of popular veneration is the small agricultural town of **Pietrelcina**, the ancient Preta Pucina, between the 15th and 16th century the fief of the jurisconsult Bartolomeo Camerario. This was the birthplace, in 1887, of Francesco Forgione, a man who would later earn himself great fame and veneration with the simple name of Padre Pio.

The basilica di Montevergine at the foot of the Partenio. Below, the archeological area of Mirabella Eclano.

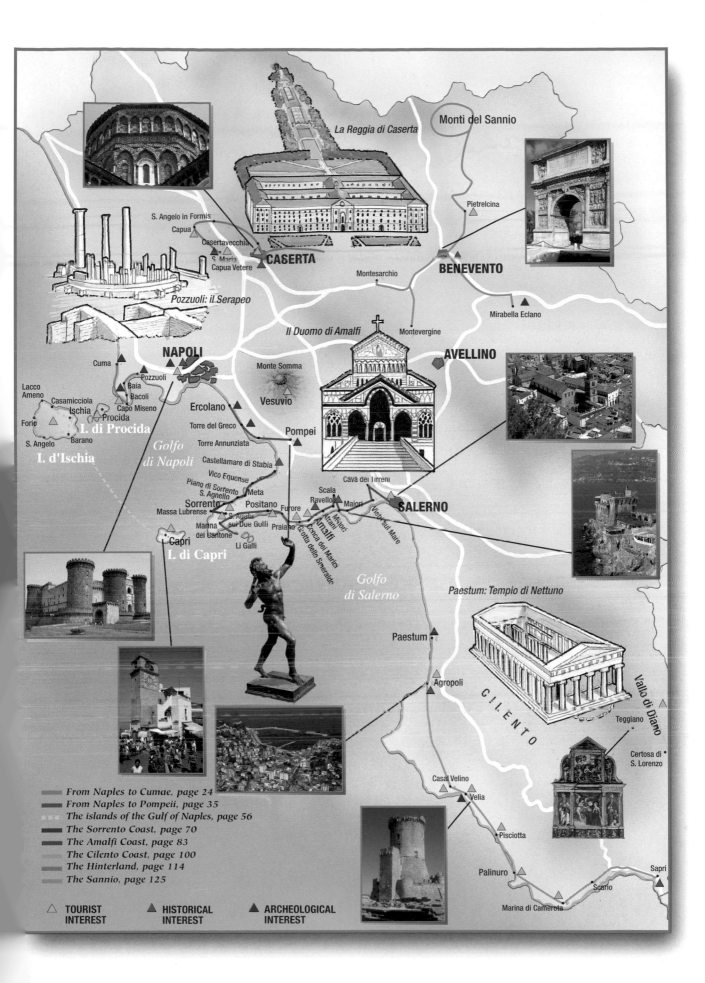

La Reggia di Caserta

Monti del Sannio

Pietrelcina

S. Angelo in Formis

Capua

Casertavecchia

S. Maria
Capua Vetere

CASERTA

BENEVENTO

Montesarchio

Pozzuoli: il Serapeo

Mirabella Eclano

Il Duomo di Amalfi

Montevergine

NAPOLI

Monte Somma

AVELLINO

Cuma

Pozzuoli

Vesuvio

Lacco
Ameno

Baia

Bacoli

Casamicciola

Ischia

Capo Miseno

Procida

Ercolano

Forio

I. di Procida

Torre del Greco

Pompei

S. Angelo

Barano

I. d'Ischia

Golfo
di Napoli

Torre Annunziata

Castellamare di Stabia

Vico Equense

Cava dei Tirreni

Piano di Sorrento

S. Agnello

Meta

Scala

Ravello

Sorrento

Positano

Furore

Maiori

Massa Lubrense

S. Agata

Praiano

Amalfi

Atrani

Minori

SALERNO

Marina
del Cantone

sui Due Golfi

Conca dei Marini

Vietri sul Mare

Grotta dello Smeraldo

Capri

Li Galli

I. di Capri

Golfo
di Salerno

Paestum: Tempio di Nettuno

Paestum

Agropoli

CILENTO

Vallo di Diano

Teggiano

Certosa di
S. Lorenzo

Casal Velino

Velia

Pisciotta

Palinuro

Sapri

Scario

Marina di Camerota

From Naples to Cumae, page 24
From Naples to Pompeii, page 35
The islands of the Gulf of Naples, page 56
The Sorrento Coast, page 70
The Amalfi Coast, page 83
The Cilento Coast, page 100
The Hinterland, page 114
The Sannio, page 125

△ TOURIST
INTEREST

▲ HISTORICAL
INTEREST

▲ ARCHEOLOGICAL
INTEREST

INDEX

INDEX OF THE BOXES